Dear Sharon & M

Hope you enjoy reading this as
much as I enjoyed writing it
Love,
(Judge) Chuck

JUDGE
CHARLES APOTHEKER

SOCIAL WORKER

with a

2×4

A Drug Court Judge's
Life Journey from the Bronx
to Dealing with Addiction,
Sobriety and Death During
The Opiate Epidemic

Published in the United States of America

Charles Apotheker

Copyright © 2020 by Charles Apotheker

Print ISBN: 978-1-09832-121-5

eBook ISBN: 978-1-09832-122-2

CONTENTS

DEDICATION

To my sons Jeremy and Lee, daughters-in-law Dr. Randi and Ariane, my wife Fran, and the new joy of our lives, grandson Asher Ilan, thank you for your unconditional love and support.

ACKNOWLEDGMENTS

This book is dedicated to the hundreds of participants helped by the Rockland County Drug Court during my twelve years as Presiding Judge and to those who are still struggling with this epidemic.

Although the letters that are in this book often tend to credit me for the participants' success, I cannot and should not claim sole responsibility for their success and the success of the program. I was part of a team that consisted of passionate, experienced, talented professionals, who worked hard to help the participants achieve and maintain sobriety.

This book also acknowledges those professionals, my Case Managers and Coordinators, Patricia Rogers Boland, Judy Rosenthal, Ronald Buster, Allison Jayne, Juan Delpillar, Harriet Carter, Regina Colman, Nicole Irby; former and present Assistant District Attorneys Beth Finklestein, Maria Gaston-DeSimone, Kristin Tirino; Assistant Public Defenders Lois Cappelletti; (Judge) Larry Schwartz; and all of the treatment agencies and counselors that were a crucial part of the program's success. I also want to acknowledge Judith Kaye, the late Chief Judge of the State of New York, for her vision and support of drug courts.

To my dedicated staff, Counsel Arielle Bryant, Secretaries Amelia DiCarlo Smith, Toni Ann Scales, and my Part Clerk, Colonel Robert Rolle. I could not have done this job without your help.

I also want to thank my professional editor, Christopher Anzelone, my wife Fran who contributed her advice and time, and Nik Nicolakis who helped me put this together.

PREFACE

Recently, while my home was undergoing some renovations, a young man rang the doorbell. He was a meter reader and was looking for the owner of a car that was parked outside. I told him that it probably belonged to the contractor. While the contractor was coming to meet him, this young man looked at me and told me I looked familiar. He then asked me if I was Judge Apotheker and I said yes. He asked if he could give me a hug because I saved his life 15 years before when he was in my misdemeanor drug court. He said that when he came into the court he was a member of a gang and addicted to drugs. When he graduated from the program, he proudly said that not only was he no longer a gang member, he became sober, and still was all these years later.

In 2006, while campaigning for county judge with my wife Fran and our friend Madeline, I came upon a few women sitting on a stoop. I introduced myself. One of the women said to me, "You were the Drug Court judge." I answered yes. She said, "You saved my son's life."

These weren't the only times I found myself experiencing similar stories. The purpose of this book is to explain my role in why and how this young man and this woman's son (and many like them), who were possibly on the path to escalating severity of criminal behavior, incarceration, and, quite possibly, an early death, broke the cycle of self-abuse.

Some may feel that this book is too limited to *my* drug court experience and should be broadened to include drug courts on a national level. While the names of the judges, team members, the participants, and the way each drug court works will be different, the stories of addiction, recovery, success, failure and death portrayed in this book, is a microcosm of most drug courts. However, there are now thousands of drug courts throughout the United States and not every drug court operates the same way. This is a story of my drug court and my drug court experience during the period 2000-2002 and 2007-2016.

This book started out to be just about Drug Court. Someone suggested that maybe it should also include how this "baby boomer", born in the southwest Bronx, got to be in a position to positively affect so many lives. So, it is part memoir.

Looking back, maybe I was destined to be a Drug Court judge with a last name like APOTHEKER, which means "Pharmacist." However, growing up in in the 1950s and 60s, I had no idea what I wanted to be when I grew up.

Becoming a judge someday was as likely as my becoming first baseman for the New York Yankees.

CHAPTER 1.

Debbie's Story

When I first met Debbie, she was an 18-year-old girl, one of the youngest participants ever accepted in my Drug Court. Non-addicted teenagers are problematic. Add drugs to the equation, the Drug Court team had a real challenge. Soon after coming into the program, she decided to go out with friends the night before Thanksgiving. I sent her to jail after a positive test at the half- way house. Six years after her successful graduation she wrote the following letter to me.

November, 2014

Dear Hon. Charles Apotheker,

My name is Debbie. I am writing you after having spoken briefly with Patti on the phone the other day. I had called looking for Allison, who was my caseworker when I first started Drug Court. I wanted to express my gratitude to you and the entire Drug Court team for allowing me to participate in Drug Court in 2008–2009. It was a turning point for me, which has afforded me so many incredible opportunities so far. As I approach my anniversary, I wanted to take the time to write to you and tell you what Drug Court means/meant to me, what some of my journey has been like, and how deeply grateful I am for having been given another chance to have an incredible life.

I am not sure if you remember me. I know you have seen hundreds of people pass through your courtroom since I stood in front of you. I appeared in front of you a little over six years ago, at 18 years old, and pled into Drug Court. At the time, I may have been the youngest participant. I remember being scared of what would happen if I kept using and ending up in jail and other institutions, yet I was unsure if I could succeed at following the strict rules of Drug Court (or if I wanted to commit to doing so). I did know that I didn't feel like being in jail anymore, though I still had a strong belief that I was somehow fundamentally different from most of the people I found myself sitting next to.

Despite my trepidation, heart pounding, I managed to quash the voice in my head that told me to run the other way, and I committed to beginning Drug Court. At the time, truthfully, the only way I managed to silence that inner voice, or "voice of addiction," which constantly beckoned me toward shortcuts, was to promise myself that upon graduating Drug Court, I would smoke a fat blunt in the parking lot. This was an end goal I often thought I had to remind myself of during the beginning of the program. (By the time I graduated, the thought of this would seem so completely out of the question—no longer because of drug testing, but because I was so afraid of going back to the dark places addiction took me and losing everything I had.)

Jails and institutions, although certainly a part of my experience, were something my addiction told me I could avoid next time because I was smarter now. I had a friend in the rooms who presented me with a concept my inner addict voice struggled to argue with. He told me that I could try, and possibly succeed at using without dying or ending up in an institution. He asked me, though, if I was willing to skate by, merely existing in a world of active addiction, in which mediocrity would be then *very best* I could hope for. That was frightening to me. I think this scared me because it took the focus away from the threat of outside entities controlling my life, and forced me to look at whether I would choose to take responsibility for how my life was going to go. Mediocre, or excellent, my choice. And for a teenager who had already spent years institutionalized, the thought of taking charge of changing my life was pretty terrifying.

Before fully committing to being clean, I took one more shot at doing things my way, and ignored your warnings about the night before Thanksgiving being a big trigger. I went to a party with a friend, at first just to go because "I could handle it" and then just to drink—since that "wasn't what I had a problem with, anyway." When I was breathalyzed at the halfway house the next morning (Thanksgiving), I was told I had to move out. Sitting on the front steps, hysterically crying, I had a choice to either wait until the following week to appear before you, or run away. I chose to stay. The result was another trip to jail, awaiting a bed at rehab for the second time in four months.

Maybe, I thought, I'm more like these people than I realized.

In retrospect, I believe that what Drug Court provided for me was a mixture of the level of accountability and freedom I needed to get clean. Being clean while institutionalized, though still a choice, is not the same kind of minute-to-minute commitment that staying clean on the outside often is. I had always had trouble continuing my success once I was free. Having a caseworker to check in with, and report was a useful tool, especially after having been in places where I was accustomed to 24-hour supervision. Feeling that there were a team of people, and a courtroom full of others in recovery, who genuinely felt happy to hear my accomplishments was another important piece for me. Gradually earning more and more freedom was much better than the all or nothing reality I had lived in before.

I remember sitting in the courtroom and hearing you say countless times how important it was to have a support group. After relapsing once during Drug Court, I came to find out that a support group is one of the most crucial aspects of recovery. Though my recovery has been strongest when I have had a sponsor, a commitment at a meeting, connection to a Higher Power, and consistent meeting attendance, my experience has been that I find my way back to those things when I am well connected with a support group who knows when I am going astray. Having multiple people to rely on as resources who are willing to talk me down, or just listen to me vent, has been the most valuable tool in my recovery.

I no longer grapple with the strong pull I used to feel towards using. It sneaks in more subtly—like when I graduated from college a year and a half ago, the only way it seemed everyone was celebrating was to have a drink. And I felt left out. I've become more comfortable telling people I don't drink. I say it with conviction, as though it is the simple and unquestionable fact that it is. I can think of only two occasions in nearly six years when I have been asked, "But why not?"

I currently have five years and 11 months clean (and every intention of celebrating six years at the end of November). I have grown into adulthood while in recovery and had my share of growing pains. Recovery and life have plenty of ups and downs. But there have been so many wonderful milestones along the way: I turned 21 clean, earned my Associates degree, transferred to a four-year school and earned my Bachelor's in sociology, became reliable, acquired new friends, regained the trust of my family and friends, established my own home after college, held a job consistently and supported myself, discovered things I am passionate about, found a kind and loving partner, AND most importantly—I've had many of my family members and friends who had once shut me out of their lives come and stay in my home and see my life here. What a truly incredible gift it is that I have been given this second chance.

I currently work as a Youth and Family Caseworker for a non-profit organization. We are contracted with the Department of Social Services to work with families that have children who are at risk of being placed in foster care or residential treatment. We are pioneering a runaway and homeless youth program next year (of which I will be the sole and first caseworker). The reason I give you this context is that earlier today, I sat in a meeting with staff from various aspects of Family Treatment Court, and listened to them discuss the growing need for Drug Courts and Family Treatment Courts in our community. I looked around me, and thought about the irony of the fact that I was on the other side of the conversation years later, and fully comprehended the need for these programs. When they talked about clients having to call each morning to see if it was their "color," and the other workers struggled to understand what that meant, I got it and smiled to myself.

I thought of how truly blessed I am that things have worked out the way they have that I can come to understand the experiences of my clients better because of my own trials and tribulations. Crime, addiction, recovery, and deviance are not just two-dimensional stories in a textbook for me. They are real, lived experiences. I think sometimes when I look at the kids I work with, they can feel my belief in their ability to turn things around. I can give them this because that was what you gave me.

I do not believe that of my own accord, I would have woken up soon enough to have prevented a permanent mistake in my life that would have made these dreams impossible for me. I am 100 per cent certain that I would have, at the very best, skated by under the radar, alone, scared, and addicted, and at worst, not lived to know how remarkable life clean really is. I am so profoundly grateful for Drug Court, and for the people who are passionate about creating these programs that successfully reintegrate recovering addicts into the community. The stigma around addiction too often perpetuates it.

From the bottom of my heart, I want to thank you for the work you do, and the second chance *you gave me.* I want you to know that it not only made the difference in my own life, but gave me the opportunity to pass that on to others. I respect you tremendously as a judge because you are consistent and fair; I respect you as a human being because I could sense your compassion standing in front of you in the courtroom.

Please send my thanks and well wishes along to the rest of the Drug Court team!

Sincerely,

Debbie

I was stunned when I received this letter from Debbie six years after she graduated from Drug Court. I had my wife read it and she started to cry. I always knew I had a positive effect on most of the participants but this was positive re-enforcement for me.

A few weeks later I wrote the following note to Debbie.

Dear Debbie,

Thank you for your wonderful letter. I do remember you. I remember discussing with the team whether at 18 you were too young for the program. I often take for granted the impact I have had on people. I sometimes simply view myself as an emergency room doctor, stitching people up and sending them back into the world. Receiving your letter reminds me that my team and I have had a *lasting* impact, and have helped people like you turn your lives around. I am so proud of you, not only for your continued sobriety, but also because you are helping others. It speaks to your commitment to every aspect of recovery. Perhaps you might want to attend a graduation and speak to the graduates?

A year later, Debbie was our graduation speaker.

CHAPTER 2.

The Early Years: My Family, Ms. Reddington, Polio Pioneer, Ted Williams, and the Reprehensible Dr. Archibald

My entrance to the world on August 21, 1946, came with great difficulty, so I was told. According to Google, it was warm that day as you might expect in mid-August. It happened at Fitches Sanitarium, which wasn't a mental hospital, just a regular hospital in the Bronx, New York. My mother always reminded me that it was a breach birth, delivery took a long time, and I emerged with the cord wrapped around my neck. Whether my mother was just telling me this or trying to give me guilt, I don't know. Apotheker legend, told to me many times, was that my mother and grandmother took a taxi to the hospital that day, leaving my seven-year-old sister Joan alone and telling her to not to say anything to *anyone* about where they were going.

My father, finding my sister alone in the house, asked her where mommy was. She said, "Mommy told me not to tell anyone." It took a while to cajole or threaten my sister, but she finally gave it up. My father then called my cousin Sidney who was a postal worker, and the two of them set off to the hospital in Sidney's mail truck.

Harry & Lena Apotheker

1913

Our family name means pharmacist, and it was probably generations before I was born that someone on my father's side must have been one. In those years, people often took the name of their occupations like the anglicized Smith, Potter, Miller, and Baker. My father's family was from Kishinev, Moldova, when it was part of Russian-Rumania. My paternal grandfather, Harry, came to the U.S. as part of the migration in the early part of the twentieth century following the pogroms against Jews in that country. My father's mother, Lena, came to the U.S. about the same time but from Lublin, Poland. My maternal grandparents, Charles and Nettie, emigrated separately from Russia. Nettie had a number of sisters and brothers. Charles died a few months before I was born. I was named after him.

Harry died at 65 when I was 10 years old. He was a baker by trade and he made birthday cakes for each of his grandchildren. He was an intelligent man, a fact I didn't realize until much later in my life. A number of years ago, a relative gave me a letter that Harry wrote to my father at the end of World War II right before my father's discharge. Both his writing style and his handwriting demonstrated how well he had learned to read and write. But, more importantly, his words showed how much he both loved and missed his son.

September, 1945

Dear Son,

Your letter arrived on Yom Kippur. That letter consisted of a few lines only. I did not have to read those lines, but I did read between those lines. And between the lines there was a lot more to read than within the lines. There is a sort of thing existing that we all call "feeling." Feeling does not know of any distance. Several hundred miles away means nothing to feelings. We here, mama and I, on the Yom Kippur day felt the same as you felt there, so many hundreds of miles away from us. It was raining that day. Mama came to Shul about 10:30 to say Yiskor, the memorial prayer for her beloved parents. She remained in Shul until late in the afternoon, sitting with me on one seat. Although the Cantor was saying his prayers very good, and it was really interesting to sit and listen to him, our minds were far, far away from the Shul and the Cantor and the prayers. There was only one thought on our minds: where is our son now? And so it kept on all day. You say in your letter you will not forget this day for years to come. I say the same. The feelings of that day, we will never forget. Living people have to go through many experiences in their life. You directly and we indirectly went through plenty for the time you were in the Army. I, therefore, pray to god and hope that this Yom Kippur day is the last of the sad experiences you went through. And from now on the sun will come up for you, shining bright and bringing many of happy days and years. And now my son, cheer up. When this letter will reach you, there will be only a few days left and your troubles will be over. Mind you, only a few days. Is it not pleasant to hear? Mama is all set, having prepared a full stock of all sorts of supplies in the pantry. Come in and make her busy.

I spoke to your daughter today. And isn't she sweet, God bless her. She told me of all the stars she gets in school, and which she saves to the end of the term. Would not my daddy be happy to see all those stars I got from school, she asked me. And I told her you certainly will be happy.

And so I will finish this letter with the best wishes for a happy future for you.

Your Father, H.A.

Best regards and kisses from Mama and your sisters.

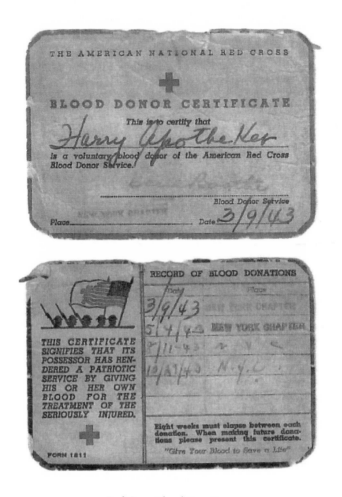

Red Cross Blood Donations

Harry Apotheker

We lived in a two-bedroom, one-bathroom apartment on Popham Avenue, a block north of the Sedgwick projects in the Bronx. It was the same apartment that Charles and Nettie had rented. My parents, who married young and during the depression, moved in with them. I slept in my parents' room and my sister and Nettie shared the other bedroom. The apartment faced the Harlem River in upper Manhattan. I remember looking out the window and seeing a tower. As a six-year-old, I thought it was a castle where the king lived.

I learned to read at a young age and was able to walk (alone) to the local library in the Sedgwick projects. I remember my father giving me money to get fresh bread at the local bakery on University Avenue. No one bothered a six-year-old boy walking alone in the early fifties. No one thought about pedophiles and my father wasn't rich, so we didn't worry about kidnappers either. It was a different time.

Meyer and Alma Apotheker

1940s

I attended PS 82 on University Avenue for kindergarten and was bused to PS 104 on Nelson Avenue for first grade. In second grade, PS 109 had just opened at the end of Popham Avenue and I was able to walk there. That was when I met my first crush—Miss Reddington, my second-grade teacher. She was young, redheaded, and pretty. So pretty that when my father went to open school night and met her, he came home and told my mother that they should invite her over for dinner. Since I doubt my father had ever extended that kind of invitation for any of my, or my sister's, teachers, the conversation between my parents must have been interesting. Miss Reddington never came to dinner.

While at PS 109, I became one of approximately 40,000 New York City first, second, and third graders to be inoculated in order to test the Salk vaccine. Polio was a terrible childhood disease. Hundreds of cases occurred each year throughout the early part of the twentieth century. In 1954, school children from six neighborhoods would participate in the testing of this vaccine. One of the six locations in the city selected was in Tremont, where I lived in the Bronx. In 1954, 40,000 school-aged children were vaccinated. We take for granted, considering the anti-vaccine movement of today, that most parents were anxious to allow their children to be essentially guinea pigs because they were so afraid of their children contracting Polio.

Polio Pioneer Cards

I was one of those second graders who participated and all of us received a "Polio Pioneer" card with our name and school. Once the testing showed success, the next year there was widespread inoculations that led to the virtual elimination of polio.

Later in 1954, we moved to a spacious six-room apartment on Mosholu Parkway in the North Bronx. The rent increased from $65 per month to $75.

My childhood was uneventful. While I was always one of the shortest boys in the class, I was good at sports. I was an avid reader and a fairly good student. I made friends easily. I was also addicted to television at a young age. I don't recall when my parents purchased their first television, but I clearly remember it being a Dumont with a 12-inch screen placed in a beautiful cabinet covered by two doors that opened. The tuner was a dial that changed colors as you turned it from one station to another. But of course, in those days there were only seven stations in New York. It also had a short-wave radio where I listened to airplane pilots landing and taking off from LaGuardia airport. I remember watching Betty White's first TV show, *Life with Elizabeth*, in the early 1950s. I was so addicted to television that I memorized the *TV Guide* and my friends would test me about what show was on at what time and on what day. But that didn't mean that I watched just anything. If there was nothing on that I wanted to watch, I would read a book. The problem was when there were two shows I wanted to watch that were on at the same time. People today wouldn't give it a thought; just DVR the other show.

My sister Joan, at 17 years old, was the national chairperson of the Bill Hayes Fan Club. Hayes was a singer during the 1950s appearing on *Your Show of Shows* and later singing with Florence Henderson, who would become the mother on the *Brady Bunch* the following decade. Hayes had one hit record, *Davy Crockett, King of the Wild Frontier*. In April 1957, he was to appear on the show *Salute to Baseball 1957*. Hayes was able to secure two backstage passes for Joan and me. Almost every famous baseball player was going to be on the show, including my favorite, Stan "The Man" Musial of the St. Louis Cardinals. Hayes arranged to have Joan and I brought to a room and we spent about 10 minutes with Musial. I don't remember what we spoke about, but he autographed the baseball I brought and he was down to earth. Of course, no one remembered to bring our "Brownie." I was also able to have my baseball autographed by Chicago White Sox Billy Pierce, Pittsburgh Pirates Bob Friend, and Cincinnati Reds Ted Kluszewski. At the end of the show, I recognized a tall man by the stage door and pulled on his sleeve. "Mr. Williams, could you sign my ball," I said. Boston Red Sox legend, Ted Williams, who was not known to be overly friendly, looked down at me and said, "Sure kid," and signed it. Until 1957, when the Brooklyn Dodgers and the New York Giants left New York for California, I was able to watch the Cardinals play when they came to New York. After 1957, I became a New York Yankee fan for life and closely followed the Mickey Mantle/Roger Maris home run race in 1961. (Maris won with 61, while Mantle ended the season at 54.)

After we moved to Mosholu Parkway, I attended PS 8 for the balance of third grade through sixth grade. The school was one of the oldest in the city. The auditorium consisted of half-a-dozen or so classrooms whose wooden doors opened up to create an "auditorium." I lived about six blocks away, but walking alone to school was not an issue. While I was there, construction began on a new building.

By the end of sixth grade, we went from one of the oldest schools to the newest.

Junior High School 80 was the next stop. I lived right across Mosholu Parkway and saw the school from my window. I could also use my telescope to see whether kids were playing in the schoolyard. If they were there, I quickly joined them. We played touch football, basketball, and stickball. I was a good pass receiver in football and had a nasty screwball with my Spalding rubber ball in stickball. But basketball was difficult. Being vertically challenged made it that much more difficult.

While I was in junior high, my mother and father became concerned about my height. My mother took me to see a renowned pediatric endocrinologist, Dr. Reginald Archibald, at the Rockefeller University Institute. When I arrived, Archibald led me into his office and locked the door. He then told me to take off all my clothes. He placed me against the wall with my hands facing out and proceeded to photograph my naked 13-year-old body. He then measured my penis. I have no memory of anything that happened after that. I don't even remember leaving his office or the hospital. I believe that Archibald did other things to me that I suppressed. Recently, the *New York Times* published a story about hundreds of young boys being sexually abused by Archibald. I'm sure that I wasn't so special that he didn't do to me the things he did to hundreds of others. I just put it out of my mind, never telling my parents or anyone else until it became public nearly 60 years later (see the Appendix C for more).

CHAPTER 3.

DeWitt Clinton, Basketball, City College, JFK, Fran, and Reporting for Duty

I became an avid basketball fan when I attended DeWitt Clinton High School (DWC), just another short walk away from home. DWC was a high school known for educating famous people like comic book creator Stan Lee, fashion designer Ralph Lauren, composers Richard Rogers and Bernard Herrmann, actors Burt Lancaster and Martin Balsam, playwright and author Neil Simon, television producers Garry Marshall and Sherwood Schwartz, and activist and novelist James Baldwin. The high school also had a reputation for having good football and basketball programs. There was a track for running that was suspended from the roof around the basketball court. If you went to the basketball games early, you could get a seat on the track with your legs dangling over the court. They were the best seats in the gym. It was then that I became a basketball fan for the rest of my life. DWC's athletic program produced such notable basketball players like Alfred "Butch" Lee and future Hall of Famers Adolph Shayes and Nate "Tiny" Archibald. But it was someone else that I watched play, sometimes with disbelief as to what he would do with a basketball in his hands. His name was Willie Worsley who was listed, generously at 5'6" tall, but could play like he was 7'0". He led DWC to a city championship in my junior year and was named "All City." He went on to make history playing for Texas Western College that won the NCAA national championship in 1966 by beating the University of Kentucky. It was the first time an all-black starting five played in the national championship game and it started a change in recruiting black basketball players for previously all-white college teams. It happened during the middle of the civil rights struggle in America and was depicted in the movie *Glory Road*. He later played professional basketball ball for the New York Nets in the American Basketball Association for a few years and became active in social work, helping his community.

Forty years later, Worsley became the boys' basketball coach at Spring Valley High School in Rockland County, New York. I found out that he was to be honored by a local college who recruited a lot of players from Spring Valley High. I was running for county judge at the time and asked the town supervisor whether I could have a plaque made, so I could present it to Willie at this function. My request was granted. I was called up to speak and asked Willie to come up. I could see that he was confused as to who I was and what I was doing there. I started off by saying,

"Before the ABA and before Glory Road, *there was this high school on Mosholu Parkway in the Bronx. DeWitt Clinton HS had a track suspended from its roof and if you were a fan like I was, you went to the game early, so you could get one of those seats up on the track. It was there that I saw someone play basketball with such ability and grace that I had never seen before."*

I felt affinity to him since he had to prove himself because of his size as I did. So, at that moment standing next to him, I said that I was probably the only person in the room that he was taller than. He smiled and shook his head yes. It was a great moment for him, but also for me since I was able to recognize someone who was a personal hero of mine.

During junior high and high school, I became interested in politics because of the new young and vibrant president, John F. Kennedy, who captured the imagination of my generation. Like so many other Baby Boomers, we eventually "did what we could do for our country" and went into public service.

I was home sick on Friday, November 22, 1963. I was watching television at about 1:00 that afternoon when the news interrupted the show. I will never forget that day and the weekend that followed. To my generation, all Americans, and to millions of others around the world, we thought we lost a member of our family. I was 17 years old and more than half-a-century has passed, but I will always remember JFK and that terrible day in 1963. If I could point to a reason for my entering public service, it was the influence of JFK.

I did well scholastically, but knew that I wanted to do well enough to attend City College, which was free at that time. City College had such a good reputation that New York University was considered a "safe" school at the time. I found out that it was easier to be admitted to City College for the spring semester since there were fewer applicants than fall semester admissions.

That required me to attend summer high school for two summers to secure enough credits to graduate early.

I did well enough at DWC to be accepted, at their February admission, to the Baruch School of Business, which was part of City College and free at that time. Why did I choose the business school?

My dad was a certified public accountant with a sense of humor. On my birth certificate, he placed the middle initial "P." No middle name, just a "P." He was obviously thinking about bringing me into the family business. But at this point in my life I really hadn't made up my mind about anything other than trying to find out the best places to meet girls. I gave accounting a shot.

My dad had previously proposed that if I was accepted to City College and stayed home, he would buy me a new car. It was an offer I couldn't refuse. However, he didn't say that he would pay the insurance, gas, or incidentals like dates. So I needed a part-time job. My cousin Sidney was a long-time postal employee with connections. He was able to find a job for me in the Flushing Queens post office where I could start work at 2:00 p.m. after school. Sidney told me that he had arranged this job with a friend of his named Murphy. Sidney instructed me to bring Murphy two bottles of expensive Scotch because Murphy was to be my "Rabbi." Now the term "Rabbi" was often used in New York Civil Service as slang for your protector, sponsor, etc. However, I had never heard the term used in that way. I said to Sidney, "How can a man named Murphy be my Rabbi? There was silence on the other end of the phone and then Sidney said, "You go to college?" For three years, I worked six days a week picking up mail from mailboxes in Flushing and then in the Bronx. It gave me money in my pocket and independence. After six months, I decided accounting was not in my future and switched my major to public administration (political science).

Working for the post office in the afternoons, evenings, and weekends gave me life experiences that I would not have had if I went away to college. At 19, I was exposed to people from every ethnic background. At such a tender age, it gave me an understanding of people that would serve me well later on.

In April 1966, I met Fran Lorber. We were married three years later. She was (and still is) a beautiful blue-eyed blonde and quite smart. I never would have met her if it wasn't for my friend Warren losing his license. We lived in the Bronx and he was dating a girl from Queens.

He needed a ride to get out there and he said his girlfriend would get me a date. Fran and I hit it off immediately. We saw each other every chance we had and we were very much in love. Fran grew up essentially without a mother, who had died when Fran was five years old. Her father, an immigrant, felt that that Fran and her older sister, Shelly, should not grow up without a mother. A few years after Fran's mother died, he married his housekeeper. Although her father may have had the best of intentions, not only was the stepmother incredibly stupid but she was emotionally abusive to the children. We were married when Fran was 20 years old. Until then, she and Shelly suffered years of abuse from this woman and worse, her father allowed it to happen. Thankfully, Fran's cousin, Tobi, was able to be like a mother and gave Fran emotional support and a place to escape.

Notwithstanding her childhood, Fran became a loving wife and wonderful mother. She was my true partner in life helping me make all of the serious decisions, both personal and professional. We were married 50 years, Woodstock Weekend. Not only do we still love each other, but we also still like each other.

I was set to graduate college in June 1968. The graduation was supposed to take place on June 6, 1968, which turned out to be the day Robert Kennedy was assassinated in Los Angeles. His death affected me as much as his brother's. It seemed that every time someone came along to try to improve our lives, like JFK and Martin Luther King, they were assassinated. During that year I decided that I would take the law boards (now called LSAT, law school admission test), and go to law school if I did well enough on the test. At that time, there was no deferment for law students and I was subject to the draft during an active time of the Vietnam War. I was accepted at St. John's Law School and began in September 1968. Having a student deferment gave me a different view of the war. I started out as a "hawk", a believer in the Domino Effect. Communism needed to be stopped in Vietnam before it spread. My father, a World War II veteran, took the opposite position. He quoted General Douglas MacArthur's opinion that the United States should never get involved in a land war in Asia. My father also thought that we should never have dropped the atomic bomb on Japan. He didn't change his mind when I reminded him that towards the end of the war, he was being trained for the invasion of Japan, which would have resulted in hundreds of thousands of casualties, and I might not have been born. My opinion changed dramatically during basic training when I saw wounded soldiers return from Vietnam. More than 50,000 young men and women of my generation, who served with great distinction, lost their lives in a war that was a terrible mistake. My father, as usual, was right about Vietnam. (However, I still don't think he was right about dropping the bomb.)

On Election Day 1968, I voted for president for the first time and had my draft physical. I was told that I would probably be drafted at the end of the semester. A week later, I received a call from a college friend who told me that he was just sworn into an Army reserve unit in Queens and there were still openings. He said, "If I were you, I would get into my car and get out there." I did, and by the end of the day I was a private in the United States Army. A few years ago, I found out my friend's telephone number. He didn't remember me when I called and asked why, after all these years, I contacted him. I told him that his call may have saved my life and I had never thanked him.

I was about to finish my second semester in law school in the Spring of 1969 when I had been ordered to basic training at Fort Polk in Vernon Parish, Louisiana. Fran and I had planned our wedding for August 16, 1969, which we thought was plenty of time since I was told I would be taken in February and would be home by June. Unfortunately, I wasn't taken until Memorial Day and we had a problem. At that time, you couldn't marry without blood tests and a waiting period. How was I going to get all of that done when I wasn't sure I would have more than a 24- hour pass?

We went to see the Rabbi that was to marry us. He had a brilliant idea. He suggested that we have the blood tests, get the license, and have the civil ceremony by the city clerk or a judge, all before I left. He would then do the religious ceremony on August 16, even if I only had a 24- hour pass.

Perfect. But one problem, we told Fran's father. He was an observant man who escaped before the Holocaust and rejected that idea out of hand. "You are not going to live in sin with my daughter," he said emphatically. He wasn't moved that the Rabbi himself suggested it and less moved when I suggested that it was difficult to live in sin with my being in Louisiana and Fran being in Queens!

He was a difficult man and made this much more difficult than it should have been. We should have just done it without telling him, but we were kids and out of respect we didn't do it. I arrived at Fort Polk over the Memorial Day weekend. It was a nice base if you were just there to visit. I went to the pool, saw a movie, and visited the PX. Then the "fun" started. When we received uniforms, I told them that the waist was too tight. They told me that in a week it would fit just fine and in a month I would be asking for a smaller size. They were right!

Not only was it a culture shock, but I had to figure out a way of getting home for the wedding. I asked to see my commanding officer who was from Lubbock, Texas. I told him I had to get home to get married. He told me that he would get the Red Cross involved, so I would be home before the baby was born! I told him that there was no baby and tried to explain what a Jewish wedding was. After much angst and with the help of the Protestant Chaplin, I was able to get home, happy to have a two-week leave. I learned later that Fran and I were married during Woodstock Weekend! Coming back to civilization, I was so envious of the guys I saw with long hair. Although I tried to avoid the "buzz cut" barber, I had less hair on the date of our wedding than I do now.

Fort Polk Summer 1969

Photo Fran and I

August 16, 1969

One important event happened while at Fort Polk. On July 20, 1969, Neil Armstrong became the first man on the moon. We were given the afternoon off to view the landing. All I could think about while watching on a black-and-white television was the show from the 1950s, *Captain Video and His Video Rangers*, which was the first science fiction series on American television. Fifty years later, we take for granted what an amazing and dangerous event this was. One of the books I read as a youngster was *We Seven: By the Astronauts Themselves*, a book about the original Mercury astronauts. From the time of Alan Shepard's first space flight in 1961, I was mesmerized by the exploits of these brave men.

During basic training, I also became somewhat religious, or at least my first sergeant thought so. Every Friday evening the first sergeant, a rather imposing African-American Army "lifer" said, "Will the following Jewish personnel fall out for Jewish Mass." We were 25 Jewish trainees out of a total of 250 men in the company. So we were able to avoid unpleasant duties on Friday night and Saturday. But how do I avoid it on Sunday? I decided that I would investigate other faiths at Sunday services. One Sunday while attending Baptist services, I ran into my First Sergeant. He said, "What are you doing here? You're Jewish." Thinking quickly, I told him that I was thinking of converting. His whole demeanor changed and became quite welcoming. That changed the next time he caught me leaving Catholic services one Sunday. He was starting to think I was getting over on him and wasn't impressed that I was sampling different Christian denominations.

About three weeks after our wedding, I got a weekend pass to go home for Rosh Hashanah. A few days before, the temperature at Fort Polk went from 90 degrees to 50 degrees overnight and I caught a bad cold. I got off the plane in New York, coughing, with a fever. Since we didn't yet have a place to live, we stayed at a motel in Rockland County. For two nights, I sweated through the sheets. My dad suggested that I go to the Army hospital at Fort Hamilton in Brooklyn. He said that if I went into an Army hospital, I wouldn't be considered AWOL (absent without leave). I was so afraid that if I didn't go back to Fort Polk, I would have to stay there longer that I got on the plane, sick as a dog. When I arrived at the base, they sent me right to the hospital and put me in a bed right across from the air-conditioner. If I didn't have pneumonia before, I had it by the morning. I remember a doctor waking me up. He had a gold leaf on his lapel and a nametag of Major. I looked up at him and said, "Major, Major, do you know Joseph Heller?" He smiled and said, "A soldier who can read." I spent five days in the hospital but was still weak and barely able to complete the required physical tests to complete basic training.

While I hated most of basic training, looking back, it did mature me and taught me discipline. Like all recruits, I low-crawled under live fire, threw a grenade, shot, took apart, cleaned, and put back together (with no parts left over) my M-14 rifle, which was always near me. However, before we entered the barracks each afternoon, a drill sergeant was there to make sure there were no bullets in our rifles, magazines, or in our pockets. There would be no "Full Metal Jacket" incidents at Fort Polk. I made a number of friends while at Fort Polk, most of who were from different areas of the country and had a different faith than mine.

That didn't prevent them from chipping in and getting me a wedding gift of a Polaroid camera right before I left to come home to get married. And that happened the day after I won about $100 from them playing poker! Many years later, I would use my military experience to help motivate the participants in drug court.

CHAPTER 4.

St. John's Law School, Gainsburg, the Bar Exam, County Attorney, Jeremy and Lee, and Marc Parris

I came home from basic training in early October 1969. Fran had rented an apartment in Forest Hills, Queens, the previous month. She went to apartment buildings in the area by herself and asked the "supers" (Superintendents) whether they had any apartments for rent. I was not aware that my cute, blonde, 20-year-old wife was doing that and neither was her father or my father. But she got the job done. I was so happy to leave Louisiana and be home.

Mom and I August 1969

Fran "generously" gave me a week to unwind. Having me kiss her goodbye in the morning when she went off to Brooklyn as a brand-new teacher got old for her pretty quickly. Since I wouldn't be able to start school until February, Fran motivated me to get a job. I found a job as a legal librarian for the Continental Insurance Company on Maiden Lane in lower Manhattan. My office was in the library. I was able to study once my work was done. I then decided that instead of quitting this job where I was earning $150 per week and going back to law school during the day, I would go back at night. It worked for two-and-a-half years. It was my first time working in a legal environment and I enjoyed it.

St. John's was a Catholic University. The first year I was there, students were required to say the Lord's Prayer, "Our Father, who art in heaven." The Jewish students weren't expected to say the prayer, but we all stood out of respect. When it came time to take family law, the legendary professor, Charles Sparacio, invited the Brooklyn monsignor to give us a review of canon law. He told us that he knew that about one-half of the student body was Jewish, but asked, "Who do you think these people will look to for legal advice about annulments, Catholic lawyers? No, they will seek out Jewish lawyers." We paid attention.

Being a Jewish student at a Catholic university had its moments. St. John's, for example, did not close on the Jewish holy days of Rosh Hashanah and Yom Kippur. I didn't think they had to. However, when I went to see Dean John J. Murphy and asked if the lectures could be recorded. He said, "If I do it for you, I am going to have to do it for Muslims, etc." I said, "Dean, how many Muslim students do you have? Jewish students make up half of the class and you're asking us to make a choice between our education and our religion." He wouldn't budge. But they did cancel classes on Halloween!

One of the perks of working in the Wall Street area was its location to the courts. In June 1971, I read that an important case was to be argued in the federal district court a few blocks away. The courtroom was packed, so I leaned against the back wall and watched the argument in *U.S. vs. New York Times*, the so-called Pentagon Papers Case. If I wasn't hooked to being a lawyer before, watching the argument in that case sealed it for me. Little did I know that six years later I would participate in a case in that courthouse that would eventually get to the U.S. Supreme Court.

In my last year of law school (1972–1973), I was hired as an assistant managing clerk for the law firm of Gainsburg, Gottlieb, Levitan & Cole, a general practice firm, specializing in commercial litigation. This was more education for me.

At Gainsburg, I worked with some bright and talented lawyers. One of them was Emanuel Baetich, a partner at the firm. I was 26 when I met him. He told me to call him Manny. He had worked at

Gainsburg his whole career and I think he started there as a law clerk. Shortly after I started, we took the subway to the court clerk's office at 60 Center Street, the same one you see on *Law and Order*. Manny introduced me to every clerk. He wanted them to know my face and name, so that when I had papers to file, I wouldn't stand on line too long. At Christmas, I would accompany him to the clerk's office with bottles of liquor to hand out to the clerks. I have fond memories of Manny. He was always available for questions. He was one of those older, experienced lawyers who were so giving of their time to help a young, soon-to-be lawyer. I would be so fortunate to meet many of them in the next few years.

I shared the responsibility of reading the Law Journal and examining the court calendars to see whether a case the firm was handling was on the calendar that week. On occasion, I went to court to answer the calendar as well. On one of those trips, I noticed a limo stop in front of the courthouse. Although it was the middle of the winter, a man got out of the car without a topcoat and ran up the steps. A court officer opened the door for him and said, "Good Morning, Mr. Cohn, where is your case today?" Roy Cohn told him and the court officer said, "I will take you right up." I was still in the lobby a half hour later when the court officer brought Cohn back down to the lobby. He left the courthouse, went down the steps, and got into limo through the door that was opened for him by his driver. Wow, I thought to myself, not a bad way to live. Cohn was an influential lawyer who is best known for being Senator Joseph McCarthy's chief counsel during the Senator's investigations of suspected communists in the United States. (He would also become Donald Trump's personal lawyer.)

I also remember answering the calendar and being invited into the judge's chambers with three other lawyers. When they all sat down, I did too. Then the judge said to me, "I didn't say you could sit down." I stood back up. I made a mental note that if I ever became a judge, I would never embarrass anyone like this A-hole embarrassed me.

When I started at Gainsburg, I met Larry who was the managing clerk. He had just taken the bar exam a few months before and was awaiting the results. If he passed, he was going to be hired as an associate at the firm.

I was working the day Larry received the bad news that he failed the exam. He was so devastated that I thought we should lock the office windows because we were on the 22nd floor. The firm didn't let him go, but warned him that if he failed again, they would. I was going to take the exam for the first time in July 1973 right after I graduated from law school. Larry took the exam a second time in February. He got the results in June right before I was to take a review course. Unfortunately, Larry failed again and was let go. If I wasn't motivated to pass, the experience with Larry gave me an extra kick in the ass. Larry was a bright guy, but I guess he had trouble taking exams. Failing them a few times would then add pressure and make it even more difficult.

That summer, Fran went to Israel to spend time with her family and left me alone to study. And study I did! I had a routine. I would get up, have breakfast, and study for two hours. I would then go to the pool in our development and swim. I then studied for another two hours before heading back to the pool. I would continue that routine until I turned in for the night.

The next time I saw Larry was the day I was taking the bar exam. I saw him from a distance. He was taking it for the third time. Although it wasn't nice of me, I avoided him. I was hoping that I would not be seated anywhere near him. The exam was tough enough; I didn't need his "karma" rubbing off on me.

While now the bar results are published online, at that time they were published in the *New York Times*. In early December 1973, Fran and I went down to the Times building in Manhattan where we could get the next day's paper the night before. There were hundreds of people doing the same thing.

I remember opening the paper on the ground, turning the pages until finding the right page and searching the "As" for my name. When I saw my name, I threw the paper in the air and hugged Fran and then called my parents. It's still one of the happiest memories I have.

Larry was not so lucky. He failed again. He took the exam a few more times and ultimately passed it. I always admired his ability to keep at it. I probably would have given up.

I learned a lot working at Gainsburg. The actual practice of law was completely different from learning it in law school. I learned practical information like where the courts were located in the city and who the clerks were who would help me when I came in to file papers. I learned how to draft a summons and complaint, and became a process server. I learned some valuable lessons as well. One day I was supposed to serve papers on a law office in Manhattan. The door was locked with no mail slot. There was a barbershop next door and I asked if I could leave the papers there. They said OK. When I returned to the office, the receptionist told me that Samuel Gottlieb wanted to see me. Gottlieb (of Gainsburg, *Gottlieb*, Levitan & Cole) was the senior partner in the firm and was in his 70s or 80s at the time or at least he looked that old to me. He rarely gave me the time of day, so I knew the next few minutes were going to be unpleasant. I knocked on his door and he asked Albert to join us. Albert had been with the firm for many years. He served papers and ran errands. Gottlieb asked Albert if he had change in his pocket. Albert pulled out a couple of dimes. In the early 1970s, that's all you needed to make a local call. Gottlieb asked Albert why he had dimes in his pocket. Albert responded, "So that if I wasn't sure about what I should do I would call the office." Gottlieb then excused Albert and turned his attention to me. "Albert isn't a law student; he probably never even went to high school. But he knows enough to call if he is not sure of what he should do. You're in your third year of law school and thought you knew enough to leave papers at a barbershop? Maybe you should be carrying some dimes too." I have never forgotten the lesson Mr. Gottlieb taught me that day! Despite my apparent inability to serve legal papers the correct way, the firm did hire me as an associate after I passed the bar exam.

During my last year of law school, we decided to leave the city and move to Suffern in Rockland County. My sister Joan, who had moved to Rockland County a few years before, was politically active and started introducing me to influential people. I worked on my first political campaign in 1973, and in 1974, as a newly admitted attorney, I was appointed as an assistant county attorney for Rockland County. The county attorney's office did the civil legal work for the county. The office consisted of experienced part-time attorneys, who were political appointments, and other full-time experienced attorneys who had civil service status, as well as full-time civil service attorneys (like me) who were much younger and had less experience. At the time of my hiring by the first female county attorney, Diana Rivet, the other young lawyers in the office were Tom Walsh, who went on to become a surrogate court judge, New York State Supreme Court judge, and district attorney, William Warren, who became a family court judge, and Ilan Schoenberger, who became the county attorney and, later, the chairman of the Rockland County legislature.

The civil service full-time attorneys and the political appointee part-time attorneys were generous with their time and always were ready to help us newbies.

One of the political appointment attorneys was Marc Parris. I don't remember how we became friends, but it was soon after I was hired. He was Rivet's deputy and he was as politically astute as anyone I have ever known. He was 12 years older than me and also grew up in the Bronx. He had moved to Haverstraw, when he moved to Rockland some years before, and became a favorite of Phillip Rotella, the famed town supervisor. It was Parris who influenced me to move to Haverstraw from Suffern. He gave me wise political advice and we became close friends. He was the older brother I never had. In 1977, the county legislature appointed Marc to succeed Diana Rivet as county attorney.

Jeremy (6) Lee (3)

In October 1975, after six years of marriage, Fran and I became parents to a beautiful little boy we named Jeremy Jacob. People told us it would change our lives and they were right. We were blessed with a second child, Lee Daniel, in 1979. Fran often said that I was a better mother than she was when the kids were little. I would bathe them and often feed them. I had good training. If I could be half as good a father as my father was to me, my kids were going be fine. Jeremy and Lee were good kids growing up. They grew up with a dad that was always a judge and when they were teenagers that could be both a good and a bad thing for them. They weren't invited to a lot of parties where there was alcohol, but if they were stopped by the police for a traffic issue, the police were generally kind to them. Jeremy graduated from the University of Michigan and has a master's degree in public adminis-tration. Lee graduated from the University of Chicago and has a law degree. Both of them married wonderful women. Both sons are not only smart, but, more importantly, kind.

We moved to Haverstraw in 1977 and became politically active, and Rotella, the town supervisor, took a liking to me. I had expressed an interest in filling a vacancy in the town court. Rotella practiced ethnic politics. The town had a small Jewish community, but they consistently voted in large numbers. In 1979, the judge that was retiring was Jewish.

When I told Rotella and the other town politicians that I had joined the synagogue in Haverstraw, they "promised" that seat to me. I was elected in November. I became a judge at 33, only five years after becoming a lawyer.

CHAPTER 5.

The U.S. Supreme Court, Write-in Election, Phillip Rotella, Town Justice, My Parents, and Majdanek

Most of the work done by the county attorney's office was mundane, but every once in a while, a case came in that was special.

In December 1977, the Civil Service Employees Union struck county government. My friend and colleague, Marc Parris, the new county attorney, assigned the more experienced attorneys to try to settle the strike. While that was happening, two former assistant public defenders, Aaron Finkle and Alan Tabakman, sued Rockland County claiming that they were not rehired by the new public defender, Peter Branti, because of their political affiliations, a violation of their First Amendment rights. Because the more experienced attorneys in the office were not available and no one in the office thought this case was that serious, my co-worker Ilan Schoenberger and I, were assigned to defend the county in the federal district court in Manhattan. The trial lasted six weeks and culminated in a verdict for the two assistant public defenders Finke and Tabakman. The presiding judge, Vincent

Broderick, who had been fired as a New York City police commissioner for political reasons 10 years before, didn't help our side in the least!

We appealed the case, but the verdict was affirmed by the 2nd Circuit Court of Appeals.

Parris assigned me to prepare the writ of certiorari asking the U.S. Supreme Court to review the case. In June 1979, right after my son Lee was born, the Supreme Court granted our writ. The case would be *Branti vs. Finkel*. I wanted to argue the case. Marc asked me to check if we could split the argument. We could not. Marc said he was 12 years older and probably would not get another chance to get to the Supreme Court. While I was disappointed, my feelings were soothed when he told me I was to come with him to Washington to "second chair" him. I was the only one he allowed to go with him from the office. I worked all summer on the brief and waited for notification from the court about the date of the argument.

The argument was scheduled for December 4, 1979, a few weeks after I was elected town justice. Marc and I flew to D.C. on the Sunday before the Tuesday argument. We went out to dinner Sunday night at a restaurant with a beautiful view of the Capitol all lit up. During dinner, Marc said that we had to enjoy life as much as possible. No one could have anticipated that night that his life would be tragically cut short just a few years later. After dinner, we spent a few hours going over his argument. On Monday morning, we went to the court to view the arguments that would take place that day. Marc was obviously nervous about Tuesday and we felt that watching the arguments would relax him.

Our argument was scheduled after lunch on Tuesday. However, about 10 minutes before the lunch break, the last argument ended early and Chief Justice Warren Burger called our case. Marc started his argument, but—as is often with cases before the court—was interrupted with questions from the justices. Mercifully, they then broke for lunch, which gave Marc and me the opportunity to go over the justice's questions and prepare answers. It also settled Marc down and he was much less nervous after the lunch break.

Our argument consisted of defending the political appointment process to fill these assistant public defender positions. We basically dared the justices to change a political process used by many of the justices to get themselves to the highest court. In his argument, Marc urged the court not to end that process and used his recent past of climbing the political ladder and the possibility of future political appointments and elective office for him. He also turned to me and told the court that I was an assistant county attorney and was recently elected as a town justice. All of the justices looked at me. Although Marc used me to make a point, introducing me to the Supreme Court was also his way of thanking me for all of the work I had done. I never forgot it. When we left, we took pictures of each other on the steps of the Supreme Court. Those pictures were lost for over 30 years.

U.S. Supreme Court

December 4, 1979

On March 31, 1980, we received the decision. We lost by a 6 to 3 vote. Although disappointed to lose, it was the most incredible professional experience in my life, not knowing what else I would experience.

I was running for re-election in 1983. In order to receive the political party designation, you had to be selected at a party convention. However, that year a new state law required a primary (obtaining signatures to get on the ballot) or a caucus. For some reason, the leaders of the town Democratic Party ignored the law. But the Republican Party did not. For generations, Haverstraw had been a solidly Democratic town. However, the Republicans saw a chance to gain power and waited until the time passed to comply with the requirements of the new law and then initiated a lawsuit to remove the Democrats from the ballot. Although the Democrats won at the trial level, the decision was appealed and the appellate court reversed the lower court decision.

We then appealed to the New York State Court of Appeals—the highest court in the state. I represented myself. During the argument, Judge Jones told me that I could always run as a write-in candidate. I said, "Respectfully Judge *Jones*, my name is APOTHEKER, not Jones." We also had a "*Godfather*" moment during the hearing. The former chairman of the state Democratic committee sat in the back of the courtroom. Apparently, he was influential in Chief Judge Lawrence Cooke getting his appointment and thought it might help for him to be there. It didn't. So with two weeks to Election Day, we were off the ballot and faced with undertaking a write-in campaign.

We all worked extremely hard to turn out the traditional Democratic vote. We went to condominiums with a voting machine and instructed senior citizens on how to insert our names (spelled correctly) in the right spots on the ballot. On Election Day, we distributed cards with our names and offices in the same location as on the machine. That hard work was rewarded when the voters of the town came out in numbers higher than they ever had before. They were incensed that the Republican Party was committing a *coup d'état*. Five thousand people wrote my name in the tiny space above the ballot. My position on the ballot was next to the slot for the Superintendent of Highways. He used to tease me by saying that if the voters had written my name in his slot and written his name in my slot, I would be plowing the roads in the winter and he would be hearing cases.

I didn't realize it then, but 5,000 voters, who didn't know I existed two weeks before the election, not only wrote my name in, but spelled it correctly. It set the stage for my county-wide election for county judge in 2006.

Phillip Rotella, my "Rabbi," passed away in 1996. A year later, I wrote this piece in the local paper:

"Phillip J. Rotella

How many times in 1983 did the voters of Haverstraw spell that name, as well as the others, including mine way on the bottom, when the Haverstraw voters endured a write-in election that November. Those memories and others came back to me as we mark the first anniversary of his death. It is difficult to feel a sense of loss for anyone who had the good fortune to live 88 years and be productive for all of that time. And yet I do feel such loss, not only for myself, but also for all that will never again experience his political magic. Politics, the ability to be elected and consistently reelected, was the reason he was able to leave the people of Haverstraw the gifts he left them and it was his political side that intrigued and impressed me the most.

Philly had the knowledge to have authored a political science textbook that generations of would-be politicians or political science junkies would have studied. The first few chapters could have been entitled: 1. *Be born in your community and devote your entire life to it.* 2. *Educate yourself on every aspect of Town and County government, including the most complicated subjects, so you could hold your own with the professionals. 3. Hire competent and qualified people, demand the best from them, pay them as little as possible in order to keep taxes down, and expect them to help you on Election Day.*

It was his personal touch—his ability to make you trust him to do the right thing, even if you disagreed with him—that was his best asset. Obviously, those Haverstraw residents who lived here for a long time always knew that he possessed those qualities. But those of us—the "carpetbaggers" from the Bronx and elsewhere—we had to learn that although he lacked a "formal" education, he had a quality that many politicians lacked—good old common sense. He also had the ability to learn and master complicated engineering and construction matters, and could carry on a conversation with most about those topics. His ability to be quiet and keep his own counsel was, at times, mistaken for a lack of intelligence; lack of education maybe, but not intelligence. Just try some fancy double-talk and you would soon see the true intellect of the man, when he asked a searching question and revealed the depth of his knowledge about the subject matter.

He wanted, and obtained, many of the smaller paying public jobs that other politicians couldn't be bothered with. He was shrewd enough to realize that it earned him the eternal gratitude of that person, his family, and friends who, in turn, made up the backbone of his political base. However, he was not only satisfied with the so-called "little" jobs. He also was able to garner the highest-level positions as well. Any successful politician will tell you that the ability to pick good people for high-level positions is very important since it directly reflects on the politician doing the appointing. In 1977, at the height of his power, Philly, seizing the political opportunities presented, engineered the simultaneous appointments to the positions of County Attorney and Public Defender for two of his favorite and most competent Haverstraw lawyers.

The service by Marc Paris and Peter Branti Jr. to county government in those positions was as much a credit to Mr. Rotella, whose political mastery helped them get those jobs, as it was to their own unsurpassed performance.

I ran with Philly five times. He selected me to run as Town Justice in 1979 to succeed the venerable Judge Samuel Miller because Phil wanted someone of the same religious background to continue in that office—some called it a Haverstraw "Brandeis Seat"—and Phil was politically astute enough to recognize the importance of inclusion in politics. He always encouraged me to run ahead of him in the districts in which I lived. He felt that if you couldn't run well in the districts where the people knew you best, you had no business running for office anywhere. But the "write-in" election in 1983 was truly the highpoint of Phil's political career and I was fortunate to be running for re-election that year with him. The story has been told many times, but that election was a testament to *his* popularity and also to the intelligence of the Haverstraw voter who would not be disenfranchised. Myself and all of the other people on the ticket that November never deluded ourselves into believing that those 5,000 voters who wrote in our names would have bothered if Philly were not at the top of the ticket. It was Phil they were thanking and paying their respects to then, as I do now."

I had a 27-year career as town justice. I handled traffic matters, small claims, misdemeanor cases such as drunk driving, and felony arraignments. On Christmas Eve, 1980, at the end of my first year, I was called out on an arraignment on an offense where a young girl was killed in a collision caused by a drunk driver who entered the Palisades Parkway in the wrong direction. The offender came before me disheveled but otherwise uninjured. I held him without bail. Later that evening I received a telephone call from his lawyer. He was asking me to set bail on his client. He said, "It's Christmas Eve." I told him, "It was Christmas Eve for the young girl's family he killed," and hung up the phone. From that day on, through my over two dozen years, I never forgot that incident and took DWI offenses seriously.

During my town justice career, I had a number of notable cases, one of which was cited in later cases after it was published. This case was entitled *Doe v. Roe*, which is done to protect the identity of the parties in a matter that could reveal embarrassing information. The plaintiff, a former boyfriend, sued his ex-girlfriend alleging that she infected him with chlamydia, which is a sexually transmitted disease. He claimed damages for medical treatment, mental anguish, and "loss of capacity for the enjoyment of life," totaling $2,000, the jurisdictional limit in the small claims part.

The ex-girlfriend counterclaimed for the same amount claiming intentional infliction of emotional distress based upon threatening and abusive phone calls the former boyfriend allegedly made to his ex-girlfriend and the alleged vandalizing of the ex-girlfriend's car that took place during the same time period.

The boyfriend claimed that he engaged in sexual activity *only* with the defendant. He *did not* use a condom during this relationship since the defendant utilized other forms of birth control. The ex-girlfriend claimed that she never engaged in sex with anyone else during their relationship.

I found that although New York recognizes a cause of action for intentional or negligent communication of a venereal disease, after examining the testimony and the proof submitted, I dismissed the former boyfriend's case because there was insufficient proof that the ex-girlfriend knew of her condition and intentionally transmitted it to her former boyfriend. I felt there was no more proof that the ex-girlfriend transmitted this disease to the ex-boyfriend than there was proof that the ex-boyfriend transmitted it to the ex-girlfriend.

I also found that a person who engages in *unprotected* sex, at a time of the prevalence of sexually transmitted diseases, including some that are fatal, assume the risk of contracting such diseases. Both parties in an intimate relationship have a duty to adequately protect themselves.

And then my famous quote, "When one ventures out in the rain without an umbrella, should they complain when they get wet?"

I also had fun determining that someone who observed a small deer on the median of the Palisades Parkway during rush hour, and for the safety of the deer, placed it into his truck, should not be convicted of a violation of the Environmental Conservation law. The "Bambi" case, as it was called, garnered a lot of attention, including the front page of the local paper. After the defendant took the deer home and put it in a dog run, he contacted the police to report what he did. Under the theory that no good deed goes unpunished, the officer not only took custody of Bambi, but charged the defendant.

I dismissed the case in the interests of justice, since I determined that there was no intent on the part of the defendant to harm the animal, that the defendant took the deer because he was afraid that not only could the deer be hurt or killed, but it could have caused an accident where human beings could have been hurt or killed.

Just a few months before the write-in campaign, on June 5, 1983, my best friend and boss, Marc Parris, suffered a fatal heart attack while celebrating at a wedding. He was only 48 years old. I was now on my own. I would no longer have his advice to help me make important decisions. Even though I knew him for less than 10 years, he would be the closest friend I would ever have. If I had to name the person who was most responsible for my professional success, it was Marc. It has been over 35 years since his death, and I still miss him.

On December 31, 1988, my father died of pancreatic cancer. He was a week short of his 72nd birthday. When he was first diagnosed, he was in excellent physical condition for a man his age. That is why his surgeon at Albert Einstein Hospital felt that my father was strong enough to survive the "Whipple" procedure. He did survive, but with great difficulty and was in intensive care for 10 weeks. Then my parents went back to Florida, where he would undergo chemotherapy. They returned to New York in October 1988 to attend Jeremy's bar mitzvah and to celebrate their 50th wedding anniversary. It was obvious he wasn't well. But my father was able to enjoy Jeremy's bar mitzvah and their wedding anniversary with his four grandsons holding each of the four corners of the Chuppah while the Rabbi did a marriage service. After that, my father had another surgery and went downhill. He told me that when he was 60, he felt that he had a full life and since he had 10 more years, it was a bonus. He told me he wasn't afraid of death, just the suffering.

Towards the end, he wanted me to call the Hemlock Society in Oregon to get poison, which he wanted to take when he thought the end was near. I spoke to his doctor and his doctor explained that it was just a matter of control. My father would probably never take it; he just wanted to know that he could make the decision. He also didn't want to see our children. He didn't want them to see him that way. We finally persuaded him to see them. Jeremy was 13 and Lee was 10. Lee thought that he looked like the movie alien, ET.

The last two weeks of his life he spent at my sister's house and was cared for by Hospice of Rockland. They attended to his pain and made him comfortable. I had never seen so much caring given by strangers. Months later, I volunteered to join the hospice board and remained on it for 30 years. It was my way of paying them back for the kindness they showed my dad and I credit them for showing me how you can help and care about strangers—something I didn't have in me at that time.

My dad had the opportunity to watch me preside as a town justice. After the calendar, he told me that I didn't get paid enough for what I did. It was his way of complementing me. It is hard to give specific examples of the lessons he taught me. Be a gentleman, work hard, and never embarrass your family come to mind. I remember coming to him because my three-year-old was unmanageable. I told my dad that Lee was disrespectful and did not listen. I didn't want to discipline him and break his spirit, but I didn't want to be disrespected either. My father helped raise my sister and me and we turned out OK. So I thought my dad would have some words of wisdom. His words were simply, "You think being a father is easy." He was telling me that I needed to find a way to manage my son. My dad was a wonderful person and one of the smartest people I have ever met.

My mother and father were much different. My father was quite social, my mother much more private. Growing up, Mom was supportive, always telling me that I could be anything I wanted to be. There was no doubt that she loved me very much and was proud of my accomplishments. As she got older, she became more reclusive. She stayed in her apartment in Florida, not going out much and thought that only old people went to senior centers. Still a beautiful woman when my father died, she refused to go out with men. "I had the best," she would say. My sister and I would urge her—"second best wasn't so bad"—but to no avail.

After my dad died a week before his 72nd birthday, my mother, at 70 years old and still an attractive woman, could have grieved for a normal period of time, found another partner for companionship, or got involved in a charity or a senior citizen's center. Instead, she grieved for the rest of her life. She could have used the time she had to be productive in some way. I remember reminding her after my father died that as a young girl she played the piano and sang. "They give free lessons at the local community college and you could rent a piano," I said. Although she had a three-bedroom apartment, she didn't think she could find a place for it. My mother seemed to be fearful of trying new things and that fear got in the way of her making a life for herself after my dad died.

She did love all of her grandchildren and often provided a place for my nephew Harry to sleep while he struggled with his drug addiction.

Mom died a few weeks short of her 96th birthday, outliving my father by 25 years. If the situation was reversed and my father had the benefit of those years, he would have also grieved, but he would have gone on with his life, found a partner, or two, or three, and found something interesting to do. My dad was cheated. My mom was given more than a generous amount of years. Life is unfair.

In 1991, I was invited to go on a trip sponsored by Israeli Bonds. We first went to Poland to visit the camps and then on to Israel. At one particular camp called Majdanek, in southeast Poland, I noticed that it was located within a few miles of the city of Lublin and the camp could be clearly seen by those who lived in the city. It was the city my grandmother Lena left as a young girl in the early 1900s. I was asked to read something at that camp. I told the group that while I always loved my Grandma Lena, I never realized how much I owed her and her parents. Had she not left, she would have quite likely perished in that camp.

As the 20th century was coming to a close, I was enjoying a great career and a wonderful family. Life was good and I didn't think it could get much better professionally. After all, I went to the US Supreme Court on a case; for a lawyer, it doesn't get much better than that.

I didn't realize then that in a few years I would embark on a journey that would change and enrich my professional and personal life, in a way I could never have imagined.

From Left to Right Brother in Law Danny Kaufman, Sister in

Law Shelly Kaufman, Fran and I September 1971

Fran, 1972

Visiting Jeremy at UM 1993

Go Blue!

Fran and I

Lee and Randi's Wedding June, 2010

Myself, Jeremy and Lee May 5, 2019

Ariane and Jeremy's Wedding May 5, 2019

My Sister Joan and I

Grandson Asher and I November 2018

CHAPTER 6.

Heather's Story

Heather was a young woman who had been addicted to substances since her teenage years. She had a rocky start and was sanctioned a number of times. She was working as a waitress in a local café, but really had a passion to be a chef. Due to her success in Drug Court, she was able to make her passion a reality and was accepted at the Culinary Institute of America.

"Fully conveying my past year in words is difficult. It's such a vast, deep and total change that I don't believe I fully grasp it myself. Coming up on my first clean anniversary was a very overwhelming experience. I had many moments of reflection, some positive, some negative. I had a moment around a week before my year where it all kind of hit me. I thought about where I was a year before and really connected with it. My brother had just beaten me up. I didn't feel safe in my own home. I didn't feel safe in my own mind, I had accepted that drunk was what I was and always would be. *I had accepted my existence to always be a pitiful shameful one, one of…and completely lost it.* I bawled on the phone for an hour with my sponsor reflecting. It was a cleansing experience. As an addict, I am constantly focusing on my defects and how much farther I should be instead of how far I've come. This anniversary helped me straighten my warped, biased perspective.

Today, I am safe in my own home. I have confidence and I feel consistently content. I'm able to hold a job and be respected. I have friends who support me. I have a family that, instead of resenting me for everything I did in active addiction, is grateful to have their daughter and sister back. They support my recovery every step of the way. I am so incredibly blessed that Drug Court came into my life and led me to recovery. I have a beautiful life today and as long as I keep doing the next right thing, it will stay that way."

CHAPTER 7.

Drug Court: A Brief History

In 1988, in Dade County, Florida, at the height of the cocaine epidemic, Judge Stanley Goldstein, with the assistance of District Attorney (later U.S. Attorney General) Janet Reno, decided that they were tired of seeing the same drug addicted offenders over and over. The fact that offenders were sent to jail or prison didn't seem to matter; the behavior would be repeated. They came up with a revolutionary idea of dealing with non-violent drug addicted offenders.

1. Have the prosecutor, the defense attorney, probation, law enforcement, and treatment on a team to advise the judge.

2. Have the participants plead guilty, so that there is something to hold over their heads.

3. Coerce those participants into treatment.

4. Motivate them to stay in treatment.

5. Encourage them to go to self-help meetings, get a sponsor, and a home group

6. Have them come to court weekly where the judge has a conversation with each of them in front of everyone.

7. During the conversation, the judge either praises the defendant for doing well or gives the defendant a sanction for some violation, all done in front of all of the participants.

8. Help them get a job or back into school.

9. Graduate the successes and send the failures to jail/prison, all in front of the entire group.

Drug treatment Court was born. And as they say, the rest is history.

What is the difference between Drug Courts and traditional criminal courts? Drug Courts are non-adversarial. Both the prosecutor and defense attorney try to work within a team framework, which includes a treatment component, to obtain the best possible outcome for the defendant-participant. The participant generally pleads guilty to the crime and faces less punishment if he/she successfully completes the program. In a traditional criminal court, the prosecutor is seeking a conviction and the defense attorney is trying his best to get his client off. Before drug courts, a judge might sentence the defendant to probation with a treatment component, but rarely brought the defendant back unless there was a problem. The Drug Court concept became one of the most revolutionary ideas in the criminal justice field in generations. Research has proven that when you combine court supervision *with* mandated treatment you have much better outcomes.

In 1997, Rockland County began exploring the idea of instituting a Misdemeanor Drug Court in one of the courts in the county. As one of the more experienced town justices I weighed in on the issue. I was suspicious whenever someone was advocating a centralized court, which could take away the authority of the local judge, and I vocally opposed the idea. Judges aren't social workers, I thought, and drug addicts who commit crimes belonged in jail, the longer the better. I imagined Drug Court as a place where the judge, playing the guitar, sits in the middle of a room of addicts, singing Kumbaya.

Thankfully, no one listened to my rants and Rockland County's Drug Court began in Clarkstown. It was the first Drug Court in the Hudson Valley. I was invited to its first graduation ceremony. I watched a woman who struggled with addiction for her whole life and had lost her children to foster care. She made it through the program and got her children back. I thought that maybe there is something to this. I did some research and started to change my mind. When it was time to change courts, I volunteered to bring it to my court. When I told the town supervisor that I would like to do this, he was concerned that we might bring "undesirables" into our town. I explained that these "undesirables" already lived here. They were our children, parents, nieces and nephews, aunts, uncles, and cousins. In early 2000, I became the presiding judge of the Rockland County Drug Court.

The first few months was a learning experience: learning about addiction, learning about recovery by going to AA meetings, and getting to know and work with my team.

When I first became a Drug Court judge, I was under the impression that drug addicts were economically and socially deprived. Drug addiction, however, is not like the story of Passover where God commanded that the Jewish people place lamb's blood on their doorposts, so that the Angel of Death would "pass over" their homes. Drug addiction is an equal opportunity disease. It affects people from all walks of life; no socio-economic, race, ethnicity, gender, or religious background was immune. Although today there is more attention made to this terrible epidemic, the sad truth is that when this disease was primarily affecting the minority community there was little attention paid other than criminal sanctions. It was only when this disease went mainstream (affecting white middle-class families) that the nation started to understand how terrible this disease is and treat it in a serious way.

I was also able to understand addiction as a family member. My nephew was addicted to cocaine for most of his adult life. He has been clean now for over 10 years. But during his active addiction, I knew what he put my sister, my mother, and his brother through. Yes, families also suffer when their close relatives are addicted. I shared that personal experience with parents of addicts. I wanted them to know that, like them, I experienced this disease as a family member. If a judge can have this in his family, maybe the shame and embarrassment would be less for them.

I presided over the Rockland County Misdemeanor Drug Court from 2000–2002. In 2002, Chief Judge of the New York Court of Appeals Judith Kaye, who was the administrative leader of the entire state court system, ordered that each county in the state institute a Drug Court. In Rockland, it meant that the Drug Court would handle both misdemeanors and felonies as part of the county court. Since I was a town justice, I would no longer be able to preside over the Drug Court. Seeing that I was going through Drug Court "withdrawal," someone suggested that I apply to the National Drug Court Institute based in Alexandria, Virginia, to be a member of their faculty. Soon after, I was approved and for the next 12 years I traveled around the U.S. helping new Drug Courts get started. Some of my experiences as a faculty member are mentioned in other sections of the book. As a faculty member, I was not only able to impart my experiences, but I also learned additional information that would improve my performance as a Drug Court judge.

In 2006, I decided to run for a county court judgeship. All of the candidates had to present themselves at the Democratic convention. This is, in part, what I said.

"Thank you, Mr. Chairman and members of this committee, for the opportunity to address you at this convention.

It has been a privilege to serve on the Board of Rockland Council on Alcohol and other Drug Dependencies where I have learned about prevention, education, and treatment being the keys to a successful war on drugs.

Running for this office since December of last year has given me even more insight into the human experience. Some think judges should be appointed, not elected. But because of this campaign and the seven others I have run in, I can tell you that judges *should* be elected. We need to be exposed to various groups and cultures, not to be beholden to them but to become knowledgeable about them. Appointed judges rarely get that opportunity and it's their loss.

My work with drug addicts as Rockland's Drug Court judge was a life-changing experience for me. I never knew my capacity for both toughness and compassion. It also changed my opinion about what is required to actually win the war on drugs and not just have slogans about it. I've brought honor to this county by earning a national reputation as a Drug Court practitioner and teacher, and believe it is my responsibility as a citizen as well as a judge to do what I can to reduce the drug epidemic that is attacking the very fabric of our country and everyday causes chaos, misery and even death to local families."

CHAPTER 8.

Rich's Story

Rich was a young man with a terrible heroin addiction. He sent me this letter from jail after he disappeared for a number of weeks. My rule was if you absconded and returned, I would either terminate you or sanction you to the same amount of time that you were gone from Drug Court. Rich was able to get his act together and successfully completed the program.

"I am writing this letter to not only express my gratitude, but to also let you know that I understand that it is an honor and a privilege to be in this program. First of all, I take full responsibility for my actions that have transpired over the last month or so. I know I made some decisions during that time that were addictive and self-centered and could definitely get me terminated from this program. Most of all, I am extremely lucky that these decisions didn't end up fatal. I have learned a lot about myself in this time, not that I wasn't where I thought I was in my sobriety but that during important life situations I didn't use my support network properly at that time. Also, during this time I learned I wasn't happy; I was unsettled, nervous, and, most of all, not myself. I was wrapped up in the disease of addiction just like that once again. I know I want to be happy and at peace, and truly be a man of honor and dignity. Sitting in jail the last couple of weeks made me realize that I am not going to get any better in places like this. I also realized being in Drug Court has allowed me the privilege to be a better son, brother, and man, and I know what is expected of me. Finally, I want to thank all of you and let you know how grateful I am not only to be given another opportunity at completing this program but to be alive. I am excited to get started working on myself as soon as possible."

CHAPTER 9.

Drug Court Process

In most Drug Courts, your acceptance into the program depends first on your willingness to plead guilty to the criminal charge you are facing with a definite sentence (jail or prison) if you are unsuccessful, and a reduction to a lesser charge with a less onerous sentence (misdemeanor, probation, community service) if you are successful. Most Drug Court programs last between 12 and 18 months. During that time, you are expected to be in, and complete treatment (out-patient and/ or in-patient), engage in recovery (meetings, sponsor, etc.), stay sober, get a job or be in school, and not get rearrested. You are tested randomly and often for both drugs and alcohol. If you test positive and do not admit a relapse before the test, there will be a significant sanction, including jail. If you admit before the test, generally you will not be punished because of your honesty, but your treatment will probably be changed and/or increased.

Drug Court works differently than a traditional court. In a traditional court, you come and wait until your case is called, have your case heard, and unless you have nothing else to do, you leave. If you are a participant in Drug Court, you and everyone else come to court at the appointed time and stay until every participant is heard. As a participant, the time you spend watching everyone else is a part of your treatment.

First, however, you have to be accepted into the program. During the planning process, prior to the Drug Court starting, eligibility criteria must be established. The team will determine what types of crimes will be included or excluded. Most Drug Courts will take property crimes like larceny and criminal mischief in addition to drug possession. Most will not accept domestic violence or sexual assault cases. The determination of the kinds of cases will often depend on the sentiment of jurisdiction (city-county) itself.

Most Drug Courts will not accept people charged with crimes of violence or a history of violence. One of the reasons is that case managers and treatment providers will be in close contact with the participants and the judge does not want to put the team in any danger. There is also an ever-present public view that those with a history of violence should not have the advantage of such a program.

Sometimes however, it is not easy to determine whether someone is violent just because they were charged with an assault. Early on, I had an individual charged with an assault on his brother. Usually, such a charge would disqualify him from Drug Court. However, this assault happened at a family holiday celebration where there was too much to drink. A fight started between the brothers culminating in one of the brothers hitting his head on the corner of a table. After carefully reviewing the facts, we accepted this person and he ultimately graduated from the program. That experience taught me that you have to look behind the crime and examine the actual facts of the case before you make a determination, and not base it on assumptions.

In addition to the eligibility criteria being established, the new Drug Court must establish an "entry" process. As a member of the faculty of the National Drug Court Institute, I participated in numerous trainings of new teams. One of the exercises we did is assisting the new team in preparing a chart to determine the entry process—the steps necessary to accept an individual into Drug Court. It goes something like this:

1. Arrest

2. Processing

3. Referral to Drug Court by police, district attorney, defense attorney, or family

4. Legal background check by district attorney

5. Interview defendant, either in or out of jail, to see if they are interested

6. Clinical assessment to see if there is an addiction, how severe, and to what drug(s)

7. Invitation to view Drug Court session

8. Review agreement, plea to charge

While it doesn't appear that there are that many steps, each one takes time. For example, in New York State, an applicant who is turned down by the district attorney's office is entitled to a hearing before the judge. That will delay the process. There are often other delays like scheduling the assessment, obtaining treatment records, etc.

We also cannot take individuals whose IQ prevents them from following simple directions. Accepting individuals with severe learning restrictions and/or severe mental health issues, such as schizophrenia, paranoia, etc., is just setting these people up for failure and that is not right. Is there a connection between mental health issues and addiction? For sure, but when the mental health issues are severe, it is extremely difficult in a Drug Court setting to have a positive outcome.

Other issues occur doing this vetting. Is the prospective participant on any prescribed narcotic medications? What are they, and why were they prescribed? Can the prospective participant be titrated off these medications or must he/she stay on them for the foreseeable future? Accepting individuals in the program that are on these prescribed medications is problematical because we test for these types of drugs. If the participant is prescribed narcotics, when we test, we cannot determine whether the person is taking the drug for the pain or to get high.

It often takes months until an individual is accepted, during which time the participant may continue to use, not be in treatment, or under court supervision. I was often asked what is the amount of time this process should take from beginning to end. My response was always, "As quickly as you can," but at times it felt like we were playing Chutes & Ladders.

Applicants view a Drug Court session and hear the judge explain what it is, how it works, and what is expected of the participant. There is then a discussion between the applicant and his/her attorney where they review the agreement and the attorney answers all questions that the client has. Before the applicant actually takes the plea and signs the Drug Court contract, the judge, once again, goes over the requirements of the program as well as the agreement.

This process is not easy and is imperfect. Some critics have accused some Drug Courts of just accepting people that are "guaranteed" to graduate. In other words, "You don't take the difficult cases." That is simply not true. We just have to make sure that when we accept someone, they have no apparent obstacles to completion, and whatever issues they have are treatable, within the Drug Court model.

After pleading into Drug Court, the participant is assigned to a case manager, who will assist in acclimating the participant to supervision and prepare the participant for court, drug testing, treatment placement, insurance, and other services.

The first time in court after pleading into the program, the new participant is called up in front of the whole group. The judge asks he or she what crime led them to Drug Court, what drugs he/she is addicted to and for how long, and what he/she wants out of the program. Most answer the last question with, "I would like my charges reduced"; sobriety and recovery are not yet their top priority. Most individuals are nervous the first time they come up and, in some cases, it takes a while for that person to relax. Having the participants interact with the judge and be able to relax enough to share their stories prepares them to share at treatment and at recovery meetings.

CHAPTER 10.

Steven's Story

Steven was a brilliant young man with a serious alcohol addiction and a history of DWIs. Participants are required to obtain permission prior to taking any trip, so that we can arrange for a bracelet to be placed on them for alcohol testing while they are away. Steven did not tell us about his vacation, possibly because he knew he would not be approved based upon his lack of progress. We found out and sanctioned him to jail. Ultimately, Steven couldn't complete the program and was sentenced to significant jail time. He wrote this letter to me from jail.

"I am writing this letter in hopes that you will understand that Drug Court truly has positively affected my life, even in spite of these recent events. In the past 14 months, I have done more to help myself and my community than in the preceding 14 years. While in treatment, I learned how to humble myself and open up to others from a place of caring and understanding. I became a leader in that community because people saw that I was making a sincere effort to better myself and that I wanted the same for everyone there. The environment there was not always positive, but I held on to the changes I had made in order to make it through.

During my stay in these facilities, I began to practice the positive habits necessary to become an independent and productive member of society. I have become proactive and reliable, but I also understand the importance of positive support networks. I have a family to whom I am closer than ever, a girlfriend who loves sand supports me, and a sponsor who has the experience to guide me through my hardest times. In short, I have come a long way.

I recognize that my growth is not complete though. I recently took a step back in my recovery by lying about my trip. In hindsight, I know that there was no reason to be afraid of telling the truth, but in the moment I panicked. It is upsetting for me to risk everything that I have earned over a moment of weakness, but that is the nature of the disease of addiction. I am proud, though, that through all of the hardships and temptations I have faced, I have preserved my sobriety.

This, alone, is proof of growth and change.

I am certain that I have these tools, the ability, and, most importantly, the conviction to complete this program. It is often hard for me to admit it, but it would hurt me very deeply to come to this point only to fail."

CHAPTER 11.

The Drug Court Team

As a faculty member of the National Drug Court Institute, I often stressed at trainings for new Drug Court teams, that your team is as only as strong as its weakest member. If a member of your team is not effective, your program would not be effective. A judge needs to trust the team and if the judge couldn't trust his/her team, the judge needs to get a new team.

Drug court teams generally consist of the following members:

- The prosecutor is a member of the district attorney's (DA) staff. His or her function on the team is to perform the legal vetting of the applicant, be the DA's representative on the team, and advise the team and the judge of the position of the DA's office on any particular matter.

- The defense attorney protects the rights of the participants, meets with the participants to discuss their legal rights, and defends the participants in matters of sanctions and possible termination.

- Law enforcement is the eyes and ears of Drug Court in the community. They obtain information about what the participants are up to and reports back to the team. They often perform home visits with a probation officer and/or sheriff.

- Probation Officer/ Case Manager meets with participants weekly or biweekly.

- They discuss progress, or lack thereof, with participants, observes drug tests, recommends placement in treatment, and interacts with the treatment program.

- Treatment conducts group and individual sessions in out-patient and in-patient settings and submits reports on the participant's progress to the team.

- Coordinator conducts assessments, assists in treatment placement, and handles the operational details for the team.

You would expect the defense attorney to advocate for their clients. Yet at times, it is the prosecutor who often advocates for a struggling participant. At times, the defense attorney privately "threatens" the client to get his or her attention in order to get them on the right track.

The hardest job on the team by far is the job of the defense attorney, whether a private attorney or a public defender. The defense attorney, as a member of the team, wants the best for his/her client, as do all team members, but the defense attorney must also protect the clients due process rights.

Protecting the due process rights of the participants is one of the most important duties of the defense attorney and the judge. It has often been said that the only thing that can end the Drug Court program is failing to protect the participants' due process rights.

In addition to my being a Drug Court judge, I also supervised 127 local courts (towns and villages) in the Hudson Valley.

One such court had operated a Misdemeanor Drug Court for many years. I received a complaint from Peter Tilem, a local lawyer who was retained by a participant's family because the participant was facing termination. Apparently, the judge presiding over that court refused to allow Tilem to represent the participant saying that the lawyer assigned by the court has more experience dealing with Drug Court participants.

This participant was being denied a fundamental Sixth Amendment right to have counsel of his choosing. The district's administrative judge and I could not ignore this violation of basic due process. That Drug Court was closed and the participants transferred to a nearby one.

While a faculty member at a Drug Court training a few years ago, I asked one of the judges attending the training about the process he uses to confirm a positive drug test. Most drug courts send the sample out to an independent lab for analysis. This judge said he uses a lie detector to see if the participant was telling the truth. I was stunned, as were the other faculty members. I had a chance to speak with the public defender on that judge's team and asked her how she let the judge get away with that. She replied that the judge gets angry when you argue with him. I told her that sometimes making the judge angry for a good reason was part of a defense attorney's job description. I routinely got angry with defense attorneys, but the angrier I got, the more I realized that they are doing their jobs in protecting their clients. I asked her whether she would be afraid of angering the judge if the judge advocated putting a participant in a bag with heavy rocks and throwing him in the river to see if he would float. If he came to the surface, it must mean he was telling the truth, and if not, he must have been guilty.

I think the public defender got the point.

CHAPTER 12.

Mitch's Story

Mitch was another intelligent young man who was addicted to opiates. Mitch sent this letter to me after I told him he would not be terminated for a second arrest, but was sanctioned to significant jail. Although he successfully completed Drug Court, I recently ran into him while I was visiting a client at an in-patient rehab facility. In Mitch's case, as with many others, addiction is a lifetime struggle.

"I don't even know where to start. I'll start with the many conversations I had with my treatment case manager about how I believed you to be fair and reasonable, and that the only people who could complain about you were those who weren't doing the right thing. From the moment I stepped foot in the Drug Court, I could see that this was more than a job for you, that it was a duty that you held with the utmost dignity and respect and would never allow it to be compromised. I admired that and you from day one. When I first got my second arrest and was told by my attorney that he strongly felt that you were going to terminate me, I got the biggest reality check of my life. Don't get me wrong, your honor. I took Drug Court very seriously from the start as I told you in my first letter, but I honestly never realized the severity of being terminated from the program. As I sat in jail while you made your decision, it was the most intense period of my life. Day and night I thought of where my actions had led me and how one terrible choice could possible change the life of myself and my family forever. The thought of going to prison was terrifying, but more terrifying was the possibility of having a felony on my record.

Judge Apotheker, words cannot express what you giving me another chance has meant, and will always mean, to me and my family. I have no idea what you saw in me or why you believed in me enough to go against the recommendation of the Drug Court team, which was to terminate me. As God is my witness, I had planned a speech to thank you and the team for the opportunity to be in Drug Court, and I was going to apologize for ruining that opportunity by being terminated. I also wanted to tell the rest of the people in Drug Court to not take this program for granted and that if (you) want it, it can save your life as it did mine. Of course, I would have been disappointed if I was terminated, but I would have respected and accepted the ruling because I knew it came from you.

When you told me you were not going to terminate me, I almost dropped to my knees due to the gratitude I have for you. That is why it was so important for me to write you this letter—to let you know what you have done for me and my family. Judge Apotheker, you have positively impacted my life forever. I will forever be indebted to you. During my drug use, there was a long period of time I didn't believe in myself. Times that I had no confidence and doubted myself.

But I know that if I ever for a moment have those feelings I can always turn to what you did. I can recall how a prominent judge who only knew me from the interactions we had those Thursdays each week believed in me enough to give me another chance at life. When others decided that I was not worth that chance, you did. As I write this letter, I am filled with such emotion I can't even explain it. When I entered Drug Court, it was to do something I could not do on my own—get clean and sober. Drug Court has helped me do that. Although I almost slipped up and used, I am grateful I didn't because it would have been the worst choice of my life. I can say with the utmost confidence that the use of drugs and alcohol will never be a path I turn to again. Even sitting in jail, believing that my fate was sealed and I was going to prison, the thought of using never crossed my mind, and this place is filled with drugs.

Your honor, I must pay you back and the only way I can think of doing that is by being an example to others by completing this program and proving to you that you made the right decision. I would also, of course, after successful completion of Drug Court, like to stay involved with Drug Court in some capacity. I don't want to get ahead of myself, but I can picture talking to potential participants, maybe during observations, and expressing the importance of not becoming complacent, people, places and things, and letting them know to always be aware that if you aren't serious and don't follow the rules, the possibility of going to prison is very real. I would like to share my experience and let them know to learn from my mistakes, and how the wrong choice can change your life in a matter of seconds.

Judge Apotheker, once again, I thank you, my family thanks you for taking the time to listen to their thoughts and feelings about me and what this program has done. I don't mean to offend you with my spiritual beliefs and I'm sorry if my next thoughts do so, but I have to tell you that I believe my higher power put you and Drug Court in my life for a reason, not to just stop my drug use but to become the complete man, father, son, nephew, husband, brother, but, most of all, the upstanding human being that I was meant to be.

Thank you."

CHAPTER 13.

Drug Court as Theatre; The Voice of Thunder

Research has proven that one of the most significant reasons people do well in Drug Court is the relationship between the judge and the participant. One of the most important parts of a judge's training is making sure that they understand that this kind of judging is more like parenting. A judge needs to show empathy to the participants, make sure they understand that, like parents, the judge only wants them to succeed. But like a parent, the judge will react to negative behaviors. The participant will be praised for doing positive things and will be punished (sanctioned) for negative behaviors.

As in parenting, the judge has to know when it is appropriate to sanction and the level of the sanction. The judge discusses the participant's behavior with the team and tries to determine whether others have been sanctioned for the same or similar behavior, and if so, what the sanction was. The sanction is given, whenever possible, at a regular Drug Court session in front of all of the participants. If the participant must be sanctioned to jail before the regular Drug Court session, the judge brings the participant back from jail at the next session and asks the participant to tell everyone what led to the sanction.

The judge and the team must be careful to sanction equitably. The judge explains to the offending participant, as well as to all of the participants, why this sanction was worse than the sanction given to another participant for similar behavior. I often explained that we treat people equitably but not always the same.

Good behavior is also rewarded in front of the group, by praise, applause, phase certificates, and small gifts like movie tickets, gift cards for manicures, etc. There is nothing more impactful to a person who is facing prison time, and has never had anyone in their life who praised them, have a judge (no less) get off the bench and shake this person's hand, give them a certificate, say "good job" to them, while all of the participants and the team applaud.

Thus, the response to the behavior of an individual participant becomes part of the treatment of all of the participants. All of the participants get to see what behaviors are rewarded and what are punished.

People often ask me, "What does it take to be an effective Drug Court judge?" My answer is that raising two teenagers successfully is excellent preparation! Knowing when to pat them on the back or kick them in the ass is important. Being an otherwise experienced judge is helpful.

Most of all, I learned that being a Drug Court judge is like being an emergency room doctor. The participants come into Drug Court broken and sick. And just like the ER physician, the judge and team stitches them up, heals their wounds, and sends them back into the world. By the time I finished presiding over the Drug Court, I recognized how much impact a Drug Court judge has in changing behavior.

A Drug Court judge has to find ways of motivating and cajoling participants to pay attention in court.

The judge obtains information about the participants from the team. The judge learns about negative things that may have happened to the participants that would have to be addressed in a serious way, such as acting out in treatment or a re-arrest. The judge also hears about positive things like engagements, new babies, new job, etc. The judge uses anything that can be used to start a conversation. I am a University of Michigan Wolverine fan. I would "warn" participants that they may wear any sports tee shirt or sweatshirt they want except Michigan State and Ohio State. That is definitely a conversation starter during the college football season.

When I was told that there was an illness or death in the family of a participant, I would express my sympathy, but also tell the participant that his ill or deceased relative would want you to succeed and not use this event as an excuse to use. "Go to more meetings," I told them; "You're no good to that sick relative if you are using."

Drug Court is also theater. It is real life with real people going through real problems. The judge has to be outgoing and creative.

When I first started as a Drug Court judge, my case manager Patti told me it wasn't working. I needed to be more outgoing—I needed to make a connection with the participants. I was too aloof, too reserved, too much like a judge. Judges usually are supposed to be reserved. It's generally not a good idea for a judge to get too touchy-feely with the participants. Hug a criminal, I thought, a male criminal to boot! But I recognized a makeover was in order. I needed to employ emotional intelligence methods. I needed to physically approach participants and make physical contact with them. The advice was sound and it made all the difference in the world. I began to not only make the participants *feel* that I cared, but I actually really started to care—like parents care for their children, establishing limits, praising and encouraging them when they deserved it, but always with that ever present figurative 2' by 4' to whack them upside the head if they needed it.

There are also times when you need to get the attention of a participant who is not doing well and remind them of what they are looking at as a sentence. Sam was a repeat DWI felony offender. He was facing a prison sentence for a period of 2 1/3 to seven years. So when he was not paying enough attention, I would take a black marker and write on a piece of paper and show it to him and the entire group:

2 1/3 – 7

It definitely got Sam's attention! It was that metaphorical WHACK on the side of his head that enlightened him about the cost of his failure.

The judge's explanation of testing can also be used to focus the participants. For example, I would explain that eating poppy seeds might result in a positive test for opiates. While some experts disagree with that view, we took the position that we weren't going to accept the excuse of "but judge, it was just a poppy seed bagel." I would tell them that if you eat something with poppy seeds and have a positive test for morphine—you are going to jail! Why, because the test doesn't state where the morphine came from and I didn't have breakfast with you!

Vicks Nyquil™ is an effective cough suppressant. Most people don't realize, however, that certain versions also contain 10 per cent alcohol. The participants were told that if they are coughing in the middle of the night and their parent, spouse, or anyone gives them NyquilTM, and they subsequently test positive for alcohol later that morning, they are going to jail! They have been warned! The test is for alcohol in their system; it doesn't identify where it came from.

I also used a can of the drink Loco, which I kept on the bench as a prop, to tell the participants that they need to be careful about what they ate or drank. It comes in a colorful can but it contained 10 per cent alcohol.

In Drug Court, anything you eat or drink may cause a positive test. We were always asked about food that was cooked with alcohol like penne a la vodka and chicken marsala. I warned the participants that you can never be sure that all of the alcohol has been "cooked out" of the food. It may depend on how much alcohol was used and how long the food was cooked. My advice was to keep away from anything that contains alcohol and read the labels.

One participant didn't listen when I told the group that O'Doul's beer was not really 100 per cent non-alcoholic; that it contained 0.4 per cent alcohol.

He tested positive and said, "But it's non-alcoholic beer." Number 1, you shouldn't be drinking it at all. Number 2, drink a six-pack of O'Doul's, you *will* have a buzz! Drinking non-alcoholic beer generally means that the person is a "dry drunk" and will eventually go back to drinking their favorite alcoholic beer.

To keep the participants engaged, I read from the book *Moments of Clarity* by Christopher Kennedy Lawford, a former actor and son of actor Peter Lawford and Patricia Kennedy. Lawford, a recovering addict, conducted interviews with both famous and non-famous addicted people. The stories were focused on how each of these people, for example actress Jamie Lee Curtis and comedian Richard Lewis, found sobriety and found *their* moment of clarity.

I used my Army basic training experience to motivate participants who were struggling. I told them that at that time in my life, I was a wise-ass kid from the Bronx who had a problem with authority. The first time I was directed to pick up cigarette butts from the parade field I said to the drill sergeant, "Why should I pick up butts when I don't smoke." The drill sergeant barked at me, "Get down and give me 25 (push-ups)." I continued to give "smart" answers to the drill sergeants with the same result—more push-ups. I got up to 50 push-ups and then had an epiphany. Wait a second, I thought to myself. If I just kept my mouth shut and did what I was told, I would do fewer push-ups. It was my hope that the participants would understand that the moral of the story was meant to tell them to get with the program—in a word "cooperate." I told them to stop spending energy trying to get one over on us and maybe they would be spending less time doing "Drug Court push-ups," meaning sanctions to jail or at the sheriff's weekend "Chain Gang."

Once, after attending a training session, I came back more energized and tried to do the same with the participants:

"Good afternoon. You may have wondered where all of us were last Thursday. All of us went to the convention of the National Association of Drug Court Professionals. There were over 3,000 people involved in this movement from all of the country and some from other countries. One of the guest speakers was General Barry McCaffrey who is the drug czar for this country. General McCaffrey was wounded in Vietnam and was the commander of the 24th Infantry Division in the Gulf War. General McCaffrey is the real deal and does not look through rose-colored glasses. He sincerely believes that Drug Courts are part of the answer to drugs in our society. We also heard from the actor Gary Busey, who some of you have seen in the movies. He basically told us that if it weren't for Drug Courts, he would be dead. We also heard from recent graduates from the [San Francisco] Bay area, one of whom was supposed to graduate next week but the judge that introduced her decided to hold her graduation right then and there, in front of 3,000 people who rose to give her a standing ovation.

One of the topics we heard over and over again were monitoring and honesty. I learned more about urine cups than I ever imagined I would ever need to know. At a souvenir shop, I ran across this bottle that you each could see when you come up—it says urine sample. I will keep it up at the bench.

This conference energized all of us to do everything in our power to help you overcome your addiction, which is why you are here. We also learned, however, that no matter how committed the team is, it is of little value if you are *not* as committed. If you evade, give phony urines, we have learned all about the newest devices meant to try to beat us. If you try to beat us, you may occasionally succeed, but what are you gaining? This isn't a game of let's see how often we can get over on the team. If you are in this program only to avoid jail and not to treat your addiction, you surely will fail and end up in jail. To those of you who fit into that category you might as well tell me now and I will sentence you to the year. Your only hope to avoid jail and kick the habit is to commit yourself to honesty *with us and, most importantly, with yourself.* If you relapse, *tell us* before we find out because you have to know we will. I am even more secure after finding out about the tests that they are nearly perfect and reliable. I also learned that there are no more accomplished liars than addicted people. I am not going to tell you that there won't be consequences if you relapse, but if you tell us they will be treatment consequences not punishment. But you know me well enough by now that if you lie, there will be punishment, and if we find out that you forged the meeting slips or you substituted urine, those are grounds for immediate dismissal from the program.

This is no walk in the park for you; beating addiction is the toughest thing you will ever do, but all of us desperately want for you to succeed. Like hundreds of other judges around the country, I took this job without any pay; this is purely voluntary. You may ask why. The answer is to be at graduation with you and your families when you thank the team and me. That will be worth more than any amount of money. So, let's get serious!"

Honesty is always an issue when dealing with addicts. Because of their addiction, they have become very adept at lying and getting over on relatives and friends. After being accepted into Drug Court, they believe that they can do the same thing to the judge and the team. When discussing honesty at court proceedings, I often recited the chorus of Billy Joel's *Honesty*. Those four verses seem to be written for Drug Court and conveyed honesty better than anything I could say. Simply, honesty was mostly what I needed from them.

We discuss the phrase, "People, Places, and Things" at almost every court session. It is used in treatment when advising an addict about his/her behaviors in order to avoid relapse. You have to avoid the people you used to use with, avoid the places where you used or purchased drugs or even thought about using, and avoid the things that remind you of using. This term is based on science. There were experiments where addicts' brains were scanned. When shown a picture of their drug of choice, their brains lit up. When shown the neighborhood where they purchased drugs, the same thing happened.

I would often warn the participants about relapse. I told them that relapse happens before actual use. I used the analogy of the place on Interstate 95 to buy fireworks—"50 miles to South of the Border," "40 Miles to South of the Border." Every 10 miles, you would pass such a sign. Just as you have road signs advising you that you are getting closer to a place, a struggling addict has signs that they are getting closer to relapse. Ignoring those signs *is the relapse*, before the use. Things like not calling your sponsor and going to fewer meetings are signs of relapse.

And sometimes the whining of the participants got to me:

"Brian, you apologized yesterday privately and told me you were going to do this today in front of the group. And I want to take a few moments to speak about conducting yourselves appropriately, and about fairness. Many of you know I am a baseball fan and a student of the history of the game, and use baseball analogies to make points about life. So, here is one. Johnnie Damon of the Yankees is one of the nicest people in the game, rarely complains about anything. Last week he complained to the umpire about a strikeout. He not only looked back at the umpire, which is always a no-no, but he went further. He took his bat and made two lines in the dirt on either side of the plate to point out to the umpire where the strike zone is. The umpire, who is actually a friend of Damon's, threw him out of the game in the first inning. Why? Because Damon showed him up in front of 40,000 people. Well, we have maybe 40 of you here in court at any one time, but here I am the umpire. Whether you agree or disagree with my calls or if you show me up, you are going to get a taste of your own medicine. I gave you back the disrespect that you gave me in front of this group. And there is a lesson in that.

This program is not only about giving you the tools to avoid relapse. It is about structure, limits, and behavior—and sometimes acknowledging that yes, life is unfair. The case managers tell me about your perceptions about fairness and often we adjust if the complaints are valid. We do hold ourselves accountable. No, we don't do hours of community service, but we do try to improve. This program for you, and for us, is always going to be a work in progress. But sometimes the whining upsets me. We have to establish standards of testing and of holding you all accountable for your actions, with a group of addicted people with diverse backgrounds and needs. This is not easy and, therefore, it is not always fair.

You want to talk about fair? Last night I was at the Yankee game and they honored, as an honorary batgirl, Polly of Candor, New York, who was diagnosed with breast cancer and had a pink kerchief on her head because of the chemo she is undergoing. She didn't do anything wrong. You want to rail against unfairness, then complain about good people getting life-threatening diseases. Complain about thousands of innocents slaughtered on our highways each year because of drunk drivers. There was an article in the *New York Times* this morning about the Irish government issuing a report that indicates that thousands of young boys and girls were systematically sexually abused by people in authority in religious schools over generations. Innocent children! You want to complain about something? Complain about that. Complain about innocent people being the victims of racial and ethnic prejudice. You want sympathy? Sometime soon, I'll have our new clerk, Lt. Colonial Robert Rolle, tell you about the year he just spent in Iraq. I'm sure he will be very sympathetic to your complaints about hardships and unfairness.

I'll listen, I always do, but if you are going to complain about something important, do it in a respectful tone and you will be treated the same way. And if it doesn't get you what you want, accept it and move on. Man up and stop the complaining. Concentrate on your recovery. Do your jobs and stop spending so much time complaining about how we do ours."

Another theatrical moment: Early on, we utilized drug-testing patches. It would be placed on the participant's stomach for approximately a week and then removed and sent out to a lab for analysis. The case managers noticed that these patches were somehow peeling off the skin of the participants and some actually came off altogether. So, what did I do? I had the staff patch me.

After I had it on for a week, I took my robe off, lifted my shirt, and showed the assembled participants that my patch was still firmly attached and further advised them that I showered at least once during that past week. I then told them that the only way these patches became loose was by the participants lifting them. I also advised them that if the patch came off, they would spend a week in jail for tampering with a test. A miracle occurred—no more patches came undone!

David had a terrible alcohol problem, but he also had a father who was an attorney. David tested positive for alcohol one day with a high reading, but swore he only had one glass of wine. Of course, we found out that the glass he was referring to was about three times the size of a regular wine glass. One of our case managers called him to come in. He said he couldn't come in because he was with his mother who was ill. The case manager asked to speak with his mother. David in a high-pitched voice said, "Hi, this is David's mother." Shades of Epstein's mother from *Welcome Back Kotter*?

The case manager responded, "David, I know it's you." You think this is easy!

David was charged with a misdemeanor that required that I set bail when I sent someone to jail for a sanction. However, the rule was that if you made bail you would be terminated from the program. When David was sent to jail, I did set bail, but his father posted the bail. I called the attorney/father and had a heart-to-heart with him. I asked him whether he wanted his son to live or die. He said he wanted him to live. I then told him that he has to be a father *or* a lawyer, but not both. David stayed in jail. Eventually, he got his act together and graduated. He just needed to grow up.

Jimmy was a young man who had an opiate problem. He came from a family who I knew for a long time. Because of my relationship with the family, almost everyone I spoke with told me I would be crazy to accept him. I was told that it would be nothing but aggravation for me and engender possible allegations of favoritism. I was told repeatedly that accepting him could result in detrimentally affecting the program. I took that advice seriously and it took a while to make the decision. I sat down with Jimmy's lawyer and the prosecutor, both of whom knew the father. I explained my dilemma. After discussing it and considering it for a period of time, I decided to accept him. It came down to this: although I knew the family for a long time, we were not social friends. Jimmy had a serious addiction to opiates. He needed help. I considered whether I had ever conditioned acceptance into the program based upon who the parents were.

The answer was no. Why should it matter who his parents are? I told his lawyer to tell the parents that I would accept their son on one condition—that he would be treated the same as any other participant. In fact, I ended up sending Jimmy to jail for two weeks for a serious sanction when he was within months of completion. Such a sanction had the effect of extending his time in Drug Court by eight months. A few weeks later, I ran into his mother, who came up and gave me a hug and thanked me for doing that. She knew he broke the rules and she knew that he needed the lesson. Jimmy completed and is well on the road to long-term recovery. His father and I never spoke about it while his son was in Drug Court. Recently, however, he did express deep appreciation for what we did. Although it could have turned out differently and caused me and the program harm, it was the right thing to do, especially for Jimmy.

Alan and Edward came into Drug Court in 2006–2007. They were friends and were charged with sales, which they described as "re-gifting" to their friends. Alan had a rocky start, but ultimately graduated. Edward was a teacher who lost his job as a result of this arrest.

Towards the end of Alan's stay in Drug Court, I was invited to a wedding where, unbeknownst to me, he was in the wedding party. You should have seen his face when he walked down the aisle and saw me sitting in the audience. The father of the groom was our friend and later told us that Alan did not drink at the rehearsal dinner. Years later, we spoke and he told me that he was still sober and doing well.

While Edward was in Drug Court, my son, Jeremy moved into an apartment in a nearby village. While helping him move in and as I was holding the door to the building, out came Edward. Stunned, he asked me what I was doing there. I told him that I was checking him out! At first, he thought I was serious until my son introduced himself. We had a good laugh and I believe he is still doing well.

Sometimes, a participant needs to hear the judge loudly and clearly; my team called it VOT. "Judge, my team would implore me, it's time for VOT, Voice of Thunder."

Andy came into Drug Court and had issues. We weren't sure whether he had some deficits or he was just oppositional; regardless, he was in constant trouble. He was also facing significant state prison time.

He was the only person in Drug Court who, when sanctioned to jail, bolted out of the courtroom and ran to the elevator. It was like a slow-motion movie. When he ran out of the courtroom, it was like time stopped because everyone, including the court officers, were looking at each other and thinking, like I was, "Did Andy actually run out of the courtroom!" Fortunately, it didn't take long for the court officers to chase after him. His jail sanction was obviously increased for his attempted escape.

The story did not end there, nor did it end well for Andy. After being rearrested and pleading guilty to a new felony, and facing significant additional state prison time, we sent him away to a long-term in-patient facility. He was doing well for a while and earned some freedom as a person who would accompany other people in the facility to medical and other appointments. He was supposed to stay with those people and return them promptly to the facility. Andy, however, used this opportunity to "visit" his girlfriend.

He was caught, resulting in his discharge from the facility. We could have terminated him, but decided to send him to another facility. Before he was sent back, I had the following conversation with him in front of the entire group:

"Andy, I can appreciate the fact that you missed your girlfriend and took the opportunity to see her and, of course, that got you thrown out of the facility. Let me tell you what your future looks like to me if you get thrown out again.

(VOICE OF THUNDER)

"YOU WILL BE TERMINATED AND I WILL SENTENCE YOU TO PRISON. MAYBE YOUR GIRLFRIEND WILL VISIT YOU IN PRISON, NOW AND THEN. WHEN SHE VISITS YOU, SHE WILL PUT HER HAND ON THE OUTSIDE OF THE PLEXIGLAS BETWEEN YOU AND HER AND YOU WILL PUT YOUR HAND ON THE INSIDE OF PLEXIGLAS OVER HERS. THAT WILL BE THE EXTENT OF YOUR INTIMACY WITH YOUR GIRLFRIEND. I WILL ALSO VENTURE A GUESS THAT SOONER OR LATER

THE VISITS FROM YOUR GIRLFRIEND WILL GET LESS AND LESS AND SHE WILL PROBABLY MEET SOMEONE WHO ISN'T IN PRISON, ISN'T SEPARATED BY PLEXIGLAS, AND WILL FORGET ALL ABOUT YOU."

Well, poor Andy didn't listen and was thrown out of the facility again. I terminated him from Drug Court and sentenced him to significant state prison time. I never found out whether his girlfriend ever visited him there, but I doubt it.

Termination from the program and sentencing is almost always conducted in front of all or most of the participants. Just as praise and less onerous sanctions are done in front of all or most participants, sentencing to prison in front of all can be motivation for the rest of the participants. Recently, one of my former graduates said to me, "You treated me fairly. I knew you were trying to help me. I also watched you send people, like me, to prison. I knew that you really didn't want to do that. But I also knew that you would send me to prison, too, if I didn't change my behavior."

Towards the end of the program, a participant is required to make an appointment with a probation officer (PO), who would review the file and go over the participant's progress in Drug Court and who will prepare a pre-sentence memorandum for the court to review before sentencing.

While this is a formality since the sentence has previously been agreed to, the participant needs to treat the interview seriously.

At the meeting, the PO asks the participant about his/her future plans. The PO then explains the participant's obligations to the probation department, and what is expected of the participant, future meetings, home visits, etc., since the participant will be sentenced to three years' probation following completion of Drug Court.

One particular participant did not take this meeting seriously. When the PO brought up the requirement of home visits, the participant, in what was described as a menacing voice, told the PO that if she comes to his house, he has pitbulls that do not take kindly to strangers.

The PO took this as a threat and wrote a negative probation report. Instead of recommending the probation sentence that was agreed to, she recommended jail as well.

Prior to the sentencing, I held a hearing as to whether this participant intended to threaten the PO. I could have terminated this participant for his conduct, but decided to treat this as a serious sanction and punished him with two weeks in jail. To some, that may sound like a slap on the wrist. However, when someone in Drug Court gets sanctioned to jail, they must stay in Drug Court for another eight months.

I believe the PO thought it was a fair resolution, which was probably not shared by the participant. However, he summoned up whatever brainpower he had, did his eight months, and didn't spout off again.

As usual, I used this as a learning experience with the rest of the participants.

A Drug Court judge rarely deviates from the promise made at the time of plea. If the judge significantly lessens the promised penalty, all of the participants will think the judge will do that for them as well. It is a slippery slope for a judge to do that. In a non-Drug Court setting, a judge has more freedom to change the sentence. The participants have to know and be reminded often what they risk. Sometimes, the team needs to remind the judge why varying from the promised sentence may affect the credibility of the program.

At graduation, many graduates looked at me while they say something along the lines of, "Judge, when I came into Drug Court, I really hated you. But now I realize that you were only trying to help us." The truth is that I really hated to send people to prison; I thought it was a failure on my part to help this person. It was my job to send those that were terminated from the program to jail and I did it, but I didn't have to feel good about it. Sometimes, family members would ask for leniency for their relative before sentencing. I would tell them that while I didn't enjoy sending their relative to prison, I much preferred that to attending the participant's funeral. Even those I sent to prison later thanked me for doing so after they returned because they found recovery in prison.

I much preferred presiding over graduations. When I came home from graduations, I felt a sense of accomplishment, especially when parents of graduates would come up and thank me for saving their son's/daughter's lives. Graduation is a great occasion to remind the participants still in the program that their hard work will be rewarded. They needed to see that there is light at the end of the tunnel. They needed to hear from the graduates how grateful they were for the opportunity drug court gave them to change their lives and how their lives were changed. The graduates told stories of their long-term addiction, failures at recovery, moments when they "got it," and families torn apart and brought back together. Graduations were obviously joyous occasions for the graduates, their families, as well as the judge and drug court team, and there were plenty of tears.

This was what the team and I worked so hard for. However, it was also a message for the struggling participants—if these graduates could do it, so can you!

By the way, *every* prospective graduate was tested the morning of graduation. We left nothing to chance.

CHAPTER 14.

Joan's Story

When I met Joan, she was a 20-something bright, attractive young woman addicted to heroin. She pled guilty to a felony and faced two years in prison if she was not successful. She was constantly being sanctioned for misbehavior and we were spending a lot of time trying to get her, and keep her, sober. She was definitely going to die from this disease unless she changed her ways. She was sanctioned to jail for a serious violation. While in jail, she decided to fake an illness that she knew would result in her hospitalization. At the hospital, her boyfriend visited her and gave her needles and heroin packets, which she hid in her panties. After discharge, she returned to jail and was surprised when they strip-searched her. Active addicts don't think long-term. The jail found her "works" and charged her with an additional felony.

Our team had to make a decision. She deserved to be terminated because of her behavior and the second felony. The team debated whether we should give her another chance, with everyone having good arguments to terminate her or to keep her. I let my team make a recommendation and I would make a final decision. I decided that she should stay if she pled guilty to the new felony and would face a consecutive sentence of two years *after* she served a two-year sentence for the crime that brought her into Drug Court. Joan went to in-patient rehab for a year. During this time, she wrote me letters telling me how she was doing and came to court every so often. She sent the following letter towards the end of her rehab:

"Dear Judge Apotheker,

A whole year has passed. It feels strange to write you another letter after so long. I used to write you once a month. Those letters were my lifeline to you at times. It made me feel good to express my progress to someone who was one of my biggest cheerleaders. I was asked to write a letter to you to ask for a Certificate of Relief on my charges. I am so happy they asked me to write to you because it gives me an excuse to let you know how I am doing!

I am asking for this Certificate because, as you know, my dream for many years now has been to become a nurse. I thought that after the life I lived, and the charges I got, that dream was going to be crushed. At times, I still feel that will happen. But Drug Court was the first step for me ever having a chance of achieving that goal. It helped me get off drugs and become the person I am today. It also reduced my charges from felonies to misdemeanors. I will be forever grateful for what you have done for me. I have gotten to a point in my life where I am just getting comfortable again with who I am. It is hard at times, that is a given, but I am achieving things I never thought I would be able to do again. I have my family back in my life. My relationship with my brother and sister, which used to be non-existent, is stronger than ever. My parents look at me with happiness instead of sadness. The doors in my house are never locked anymore because they are no longer scared I will steal anything. I am able to lend them money now and I am trusted again!

I have been working very hard to get into the nursing program and make a life for myself. Well, it happened! I am starting at the nursing program at Rockland Community College next week.

I will be only going part-time because I work full-time at an Urgent Care Center. I supervise nine people who I manage and train. I love what I do!

There have been times when heroin addicts come in with illnesses and seeking drugs. I have such compassion for them because I've been there. I wish I could help them, but I can't. If it does anything for me, it reminds me how lucky I am to have gotten past the worst part, which is the first year. Going to school and working full-time will be a bit of a challenge for me. It will mean no social life, but that's OK; I've had enough "adventures" in life. I have to admit I'm really scared. I'm afraid I won't be able to handle the schoolwork, the pressure, the stress. I don't do well with stress. I see so many people fail out; it scares me to death. I'm hoping I'll be OK.

So, once again I'm asking for your help in getting this Certificate for when I graduate. Maybe it will help in getting a job even though I may still have charges on my record. My biggest fear is that I will go through all the schooling, sweat, and tears and not be able to find a job. I am asking for your help, so I might be able to fulfill my dream.

Thank you for everything you have done for me. You have given me the ability to find myself. Not a lot of people get that opportunity. You never gave up on me when I gave up on myself. If there was some way to repay you, I would. But maybe, by becoming this person I have dreamed of, will be enough.

Love, Joan"

I saw a change in her after a few months away. After the year away, she came back and has been sober ever since. Not only was she asked to be a guest speaker at a Drug Court graduation, which is quite an honor, but she attended and graduated from nursing school while working. She invited my wife and I to her graduation and gave me a big hug after the ceremony. She is currently employed as a nurse of a local hospital. I wrote a letter on her behalf to the state licensing board. Notwithstanding her charges in two states, the state licensing board issued her a nursing license.

If you saw Joan when she entered Drug Court and saw her at her graduation, you would never think it was the same person.

Someone once asked me the reason for the overall success of the Drug Court program. The answer is that I don't really know. I refer to it as "fairy dust," which we sprinkle on all of the participants.

What I have dubbed "fairy dust" consists of 25 years of research in the best practices and decades of research on brain disease, as well as years of developing medications (MATS), which can be effectively utilized to help addicts deal with their addictions while having a normal life. And when someone overdoses, the police and EMTs have the use of Narcan to literally bring people back to life.

We have made great strides in this area over the last 25 years. But after all of this research, there is still no *satisfying* answer as to why what we do in the courtroom and in treatment with our participants works in the majority of cases, but not all.

CHAPTER 15.

Failures: Termination, Recidivism, Incarceration, and Worse

A wise social worker/probation officer, Patti Rogers Boland, told me when I first started, "Unless you want to burn out, don't get too excited about the successes and too depressed about the failures." Easier said than done!

One of the first tragic failures was Arnold. He was a young man who became addicted to opiates, not in the traditional way, but because of a serious dog bite that resulted in a lengthy hospital stay. He was also taking courses at the community college in chemistry. He struggled with his sobriety in Drug Court but seemed to be on the right track. We had a court session on Thursday at lunchtime. Arnold knew how long opiates stayed in his system. He also knew that if he used after court on Thursday, and either did not get called for a random drug test over the weekend or he blew it off, he wouldn't be tested until Monday, when the drugs would be out of his system. He went up to Orange County to a friend's house. He was found the next morning dead from an overdose.

I addressed his death at the next court appearance.

"We asked all of you to be here today, even the ones that weren't scheduled, because we want to discuss the seriousness of the disease of addiction. Sometimes I joke around with you, but I'm deadly serious now. For the first time since we started the Drug Court, a participant has died. Most, if not all, of you are aware that Arnold died last Thursday night, hours after he left court, in what seems to me to be clearly a drug-related incident. Although the coroner's report will take some time to confirm this, those of you who knew Arnold don't need that confirmation. This has had a tremendous effect on the Drug Court team and on many of you.

The disease of addiction is a very dangerous illness. It hurts those addicted in many ways, and, sometimes, it takes their lives. Although we are all aware of this, it doesn't seem as real until it hits home. Every one of you is at risk for relapse and ultimately at risk of losing your life if you pick up. What we do here in Drug Court may, at times, seem tough, but what we are trying to do is help you keep from being hurt further by this lethal disease. While we don't enjoy sanctioning any of you, I will do so to help keep you focused on your recovery. I'd rather send you to jail than attend your funeral.

Those of you who attended the wake or funeral service were able to see just how many people are affected by one person's addiction. Each of you has people who love and care about you. Your decision to come into Drug Court was the first step in your recovery and we, and they, have been able to see some of the changes you have made so far. More doors will continue to open up for you and your loved ones as you move ahead in your recovery. Even in their grief, Arnold's parents thanked us for trying to help him.

If Arnold's death can serve any purpose at all, it should motivate some of you to stop denying your addiction and wasting this energy on trying to get over on us, and hopefully make you serious about recovery. Maybe that's the best way we can remember him.

Those of you who were there last week may remember the last words I said to Arnold— People, Places, and Things. For those of you who are interested, Patti will have a discussion after court to talk about your feelings and concerns regarding this or you can talk about it as you come up.

Next week we are all going to a conference, so there will be no court. But treatment will be taking urines and the police will be calling you in for drug tests. If you want to take this opportunity to use, I guess you can. You can take a chance like Arnold probably did and try to figure the odds of getting caught and, like Arnold, the chemistry major, try to figure out how much of this or that drug you could mix with this or that medication.

After all, you're probably smarter than Arnold was. If you think you're that smart, just remember how smart Arnold was and where he is now."

No matter what happened, we used it as an opportunity to educate. Tragedies are sad, but we as a team always used them to make a point. Although Arnold's parents were still grieving, they sent me the following note:

"Judge Apotheker, There are no words to express our sorrow right now and there are not enough words to express how we feel towards you. You were kind to Arnold and you cared about him—he knew this and so did we. The tears will subside and the hurt will ease, but we will never forget your kindness."

I was moved by the letter and how thankful they were, but I also clearly recognized losing a child, especially that way, is something Arnold's parents will carry for the rest of their lives.

Another tragic failure of a young participant was Alice, a beautiful young girl addicted to heroin. She came into drug court and pled guilty to a felony and was looking at one year in state prison. We sent her to detox where she walked out the door within a few hours. I issued a warrant and she was picked up. I sent her to jail for a few weeks to see if that might have the desired result. I told her that we would send her away to a long-term facility, but if she left, I would sentence her to that one-year promise. After spending a few weeks in jail where she detoxed from her "vacation", we sent her to a long-term facility. Again, she left soon after she arrived. I again issued a warrant and she was sent to jail to await sentencing as promised. I sentenced her to one year in prison where, apparently, she stayed sober and behaved so well that they saw fit to release her on parole after serving seven months.

Within one week of her release, she was dead from an overdose!

We did everything we could to motivate her, but the combination of her youth and her addiction was too much. She was 20 years old.

Harriet was the ex-wife of a celebrity. She was addicted to substances and she was in my misdemeanor court looking at one year in local jail.

You could see that at one time she was a beautiful woman, but years addicted to substances often affect the way you look —and in her case it certainly did. I was going to put her in jail for the weekend on a sanction but she persuaded me not to over the demonstrative opposition of my team. She convinced me that there would be no one to feed her two dogs. Addicts can be quite persuasive, especially to a somewhat inexperienced (at that time) Drug Court judge.

Later on, she tested positive, but swore she didn't use and certainty didn't use that particular drug. Because she denied use, we sent the sample to a lab while she stayed out of jail, with the understanding that if it came back confirmed positive, she would spend the following weekend in jail.

This story ends with a conclusion that would make Kafka and O'Henry proud. We found out that she was telling the truth, sort of. She didn't use that particular drug but borrowed urine from another person who did use. Even though urine tests are observed, she managed to secrete the borrowed urine in a condom placed in a body cavity and used a sharp fingernail to pierce the condom to give the sample.

The moral of that story is if you are going to borrow urine don't borrow it from a drug addict!

After all of this and more, the team was faced with a decision as to whether to terminate her from the program. I wrote the following memo to the team for them to consider:

"I had a chance to review her file this morning and have a lot of misgivings about giving her 'one last chance.' According to Sister Conway, Harriet has continually disregarded their rules, is deceptive, dishonest, disregards authority, disregards the safety and well-being of others, and has no personal discipline over her impulses. The Case Manager's notes show that she was warned in December that she had a month to start to change. This, of course, was in addition to being thrown out of the first in-patient facility.

Can we be *reasonably* sure that even if we allow her to be placed in another facility she will change? Do we have any *realistic* reason to believe that she won't continue to get over on her new psychiatrist and obtain meds that are contra-indicated for addicts? Are we not only doing a disservice to her but, more importantly, to all of the other participants, most of whom probably know that she has been given more chances than she deserves *and maybe more than they would ever get*? Is she getting these chances because of her 'celebrity' status? Has she gotten over on us, too, and do the other participants realize that more than we do? I pose these questions for all of you to ponder over the next two weeks, not to criticize anyone for what has happened but to make sure (as much as we can) that we are doing the right thing. See you all in two weeks."

Self-examination and self-criticism are the hallmark of a well-functioning Drug Court. No Drug Court program is perfect; mistakes are made. However, it is important to make sure that the same mistake is not repeated.

Drug Court is constantly faced with the decision to pull the plug or give the participant another chance. Harriet was an example of probably too many chances. The problem is knowing when to pull the plug. Sometimes, waiting is the answer. Sometimes it's not. This is not science.

Stuart was a young man with a heroin addiction. He was charged with a sale, but we took him in over the strenuous objection of a local police department. They thought he was more of a seller than user. Because I wasn't sure we weren't making a mistake, we made the down-side sentence five years, which is significantly more than normal. If he completed the program, his felony would be reduced to a misdemeanor and he would be sentenced to probation. He agreed to the alternative dispositions. I warned him from the time he came in that if he used, we wouldn't terminate him, but if he sold or had enough drugs to be charged with possession with intent to sell, he would be terminated and sentenced to the promised five-year state prison sentence.

A month or two later, he was arrested for possession with intent to sell. I did sentence him as promised.

We also took in the son of a former local police chief. Peter was severely addicted to opiates. He had a rocky start but seemed to be doing well, staying sober, and chairing Narcotics Anonymous meetings. That's why we were shocked one morning to find out that Peter was found dead behind a shopping center. We never found out the cause of death, but Peter, being a heroin addict, certainly led us to believe that his death was not due to natural causes.

Donald was an alcoholic. When he came into Drug Court, I asked him to tell everyone a little bit about himself, as I did with every new participant. He proceeded to tell everyone that, as a young boy, he was abused by a priest. *Too Much Information*, I thought to myself. Often those who become addicted having experienced trauma of one kind or another that cause them to self-medicate with alcohol and/or drugs. Usually, they disclose the particulars of that trauma at treatment or with their case manager. It is rare to hear about that in open court. Usually, the team will tell the judge that the participant experienced trauma, so the judge knows what questions and topics to keep away from. The judge doesn't need to know what kind of trauma, just that there was trauma.

Donald ultimately graduated but continued to relapse and get into trouble. Sadly, he later died of an overdose. A few months prior to his death I asked him to write his story. He only sent me part of it, about how he started using…

"I can't remember anything of my formative years prior to the time I was six years old. I remember it was probably the winter of 1965 and we were living in a house in New City, New York, on Main Street and a car came roaring up the driveway and I was just getting ready for bed and my pants were down around my ankles and I ran over to the window and I hit my head on the radiator. I received six stitches and still have the scar on my forehead till this day!

Before my mother could take me to the hospital by taxi, I sat there in complete horror from my window watching my father getting thrown from the backseat of a Cadillac passed out in the driveway drunk.

The first time I ever picked up a drink, it was Friday night open gym at my junior high school. My friend Darlene had taken a bottle of Seagram Seven from her father's liquor cabinet, and me and my friend Brian tried to prove to her who was the better man and I proceeded to drink half the bottle, getting sick and passing out! I hated it but I love the way it made me feel. I didn't drink again until I was about 15. It was a horrible experience for me and it kind of straightened me out temporarily. I would sit in the back of my friend's car. They would drink beers and I would pour mine out into the carpet. I think the reason why I didn't want to drink at this point is because I saw what it was doing to my father and to my family and to me personally. His alcoholism at this point was completely out of control and I would have to say 98 per cent of the reason why I didn't drink until that point was because I saw what it did to him!

From the time I was 15 up until the time I was 18 years old, I would drink here and there but I would do crazy things like break into homes, steal things, and give the money to my friends, so they would like me. By the time I was 18 years old, I was sentenced to two to six years in state prison because I was at a bar with a friend of mine. We got drunk and we robbed a local gas station for $80 to go get more beer! Looking back, I remember specifically not caring that I was locked up and I was in prison. Just seem to make no difference to me at all."

Drug Courts participants are high-risk. If they are not high-risk, they don't belong in Drug Court. Therefore, there is always a risk of one of our participants having an accident because of alcohol or drugs. Every Drug Court knows that it may happen, causing the program to have negative publicity.

Our Drug Court experienced one of those tragedies in July 2013, not long after John graduated. He was a model participant. In addition to not having any sanctions during his time in Drug Court, he was working towards his master's degree in business while holding down a full-time job, going to drug court, treatment, etc.

On a dark July evening, John and some friends, who would soon be celebrating their wedding, had drinks at a local restaurant on the Hudson River. Afterward, they boarded John's boat and drove near the construction of the new Tappan Zee Bridge. John reportedly drove at a high rate of speed, causing the boat to collide with a barge near the bridge. John had alcohol and cocaine in his system. John's closest friends, the bride-to-be and the best man, were thrown overboard, and died.

I heard about the accident on the evening news, but did not know the particulars until the next morning when I received a call from the assistant district attorney assigned to Drug Court. The team and I were stunned! John would be the absolutely last person we would think could do something like that. Immediately, I went through a period of second-guessing about what we did or didn't do with him during his time in Drug Court. Did he fly under the radar? Did we miss signs of his use or weren't able to catch him on a drug test? We went through his file to see if we missed anything. Although we test randomly and frequently, it is possible, unlikely but possible, to go through 18 months occasionally using, and be lucky enough to test clean.

We came to the conclusion that it was possible that we missed some signs, but it was also possible that John was clean during his time in Drug Court but somehow relapsed and went back to using.

Since he was not in Drug Court at the time of the accident, the press did not report that John was a graduate.

He was sentenced to jail by another judge and he has to live with what he caused for the rest of his life.

Recently, I interviewed John. He came into the program facing a felony possession of cocaine. His mindset, like most participants coming in, was to be successful, so the felony would be reduced to a misdemeanor.

Q: John, after the accident I reviewed your file and confirmed that you were never sanctioned, which is amazing since most participants are sanctioned. Am I correct?

John: Yes, I was never sanctioned and never tested positive on a drug or alcohol test.

Q: Were you sober during your time in Drug Court or were you just lucky in that we didn't catch you?

John: I remained sober for my entire time. Even though I didn't have a problem with alcohol, when I drank, it led to my using cocaine. So, I just stopped drinking while in Drug Court.

Q: After graduation, did you continue to attend self-help meetings and have a sponsor?

John: I did for a little while then I stopped completely.

Q: How long after graduation did you remain sober?

John: 8-10 months

Q: Looking back, do you think that if you continued to attend self-help that the accident may not have happened?

John: Yes, AA [Alcoholics Anonymous] works and if I continued with the meetings and sponsor, my chances of staying sober would increase and possibly that accident wouldn't have happened.

Q: Besides going to jail, what else happened as a result of the accident?

John: I lost my two closest friends. If someone said I would be sentenced to life imprisonment but my friends would be alive, I would gladly take it to have them back. The only positive thing that happened was that I reconnected with God and that my wife stuck with me.

Q: What are you doing now?

John: I have a very successful business and have a new son. Maybe it was God's plan to go through this terrible time and find recovery.

Q: When was the last time you had a drink?

John: I have remained sober since the night of the accident. If I am at a restaurant with friends and they are drinking and they ask me to join them, I decline. I'm not shy about explaining how alcohol has detrimentally affected my life. I plan on never drinking again.

Q: What advice would you give Drug Court graduates?

John: Obviously keep going to meetings to maintain your sobriety.

We told the participants that even if you graduate, you still have to *practice* recovery.

John's story is a stark reminder that even after successfully completing Drug Court, you still need to go to meetings, call your sponsor, and, of course, People, Places, and Things.

John learned that lesson the hard way.

CHAPTER 16.

Bernie's Story

Before and Now

"When I began my journey at treatment, I was numb, scared, confused, and hurt. I was a shell going through the motions of what I had to do each day to survive, to stay out of jail. I was lost and had no direction. I had just gotten out of detox, started Drug Court with the SCRAM™ ["Secure Continuous Remote Alcohol Monitoring"] on my ankle, and was just served with divorce papers. I didn't know how to handle my feelings and emotions with no drink to drown them in. The only thing I knew was that if I didn't do Drug Court, I would never be sober. After this relapse, I didn't have the strength or determination to do it alone. I only knew that to live my life, to save my life, I had to be sober. This relapse brought me to my knees and for the first time in my life, I didn't know whether I wanted to live or die.

I remember being so scared to have the SCRAM™ bracelet put on. I felt that I was losing my freedom, like being caught in a trap. A trap, as it turned out, that helped save my life. More tests were to come—my brother-in-law almost dying, my entire computer hard drive crashing, low creatinine levels [which, in the case of addicts, could mean that they are drinking too much water to flush their system], and a positive tox for alcohol. With the help of God and the SCRAM™, I didn't drink through any of it, but felt every painful, uncomfortable emotion I experienced. I remember many sleepless nights where I fell on my knees and prayed to God to give me strength to get through it. I remember my case managers telling me that I could get through it. "Just feel it, walk through it, you are not alone." I did and I slowly I began to heal.

I learned to live one day at a time and accept what was reality and have faith that God would pick me up and carry me through. I used the third step over and over again—let go and let God. I learned how to have humility for this disease and accept I will never control it or life, and my addiction is with me to the end. Amazingly, I was thankful for the SCRAM™ bracelet and it became my new best friend.

I am almost five months sober now and I have changed and grown. I have been given the gift of life and I will celebrate the opportunities it gives me. I can now laugh, listen to music, play my piano. Each day is a new beginning and each moment will give me the opportunity to let go of all that has trapped me in the past. I am free. I will respond to life, trust my instincts, and trust the process to bring me the highest good. I deserve the best and I accept it now.

I choose to accept life on life's terms and move from the old to the new with joy and ease. I will accept the gift of change, and trust that the pain of growth is necessary for the joy of tomorrow. I have been granted a new beginning, a new chapter on life. I will forgive others and, more importantly, forgive myself, and release this heavy burden from my sole.

I am a kind compassionate, gentle, loving person. I will now move to a better place and I am joyous, happy and free. God grants me a daily reprieve and will provide the wisdom, strength, and courage to live each day in acceptance and serenity.

I am forever grateful."

CHAPTER 17.

Continuing Education and Training

In 2000, I attended training at the National Judicial College in Reno, Nevada, where I took courses in psychopharmacology—the study of how different drugs affect the brain. You learn the different pathways that drugs are introduced, how different drugs affect the brain, and for how long when, for example, swallowed, snorted, injected, etc.

Simply, how does the "high" happen and for how long?

As a faculty member of the National Drug Court Institute (NDCI), I attended numerous training events over 15 years.

At one such training, a representative from the New York State's Office of Substance Abuse Services, while speaking about how different drugs affect the brain's pleasure centers, abruptly stopped the lecture. All of a sudden, we were listening to Al Green's popular song, *Let's Stay Together*. Two hundred people in the room found themselves moving to that wonderful music. The point of that exercise is that a lot of other things stimulate the pleasure centers of the brain, e.g., food, music, sex, etc. That is why there is a connection between music and exercise. The more you connect with the music, the harder you will work. It's science!

Olivia Newton John and Jane Fonda figured that out in the early 1980s when they added music to exercise videos.

Training also included classes in cultural competence, which is critical. The judge is raised in a certain social-ethnic environment. The participants were raised in many different ethnic and cultural environments, each with its own way of communicating to strangers. For example, certain groups are raised not to share any personal information with non-family members. Treatment providers and the judge need to know that and learn techniques to break through those barriers in order to help the addicted participants. At one such training, I was assigned to a new Drug Court team from rural Mississippi. Guy Wheeler, a treatment person from South Florida, gave a lecture on cultural competence. He told a story about the time his Drug Court judge lost a parent. Wheeler attended the funeral. Wheeler is an African-American man. His judge was Jewish. Wheeler told me that at the funeral he was handed a "beanie" to put on his head. He was unfamiliar with it. I explained to him that the Jewish faith requires men to cover their heads with yarmulkes during prayers. The story made the point about understanding that different faiths have different customs—even if they lived in the same community.

Trainings also include classes in sanctions and incentives. When participants come into Drug Court, they may still be under the influence and/or their brains are still affected. They may not yet be able to follow complicated directions. If they don't have the capacity, how do you deal with them as opposed to someone in the program for a long time and commits the same offense? Do you deal with a participant who has a low IQ the same way you deal with a person with a higher IQ? The participant with the lower IQ may not be able absorb the information in the same way.

Different negative behaviors require different sanctions. Being late to court or to treatment requires a sanction by the judge, but should it be jail or community service for the first time? A participant who gets re-arrested for a serious crime deserves to automatically go to jail immediately, or do the facts of the new crime require more patience and a closer look? These issues and more are discussed at such trainings.

Applying sanctions depends on the facts of each case and its possible effect on the other participants.

The research shows that the court needs to address the behaviors promptly and the sanctions need to be graduated. Usually, when someone is late to court, the judge notices it and addresses it right then and there. The participant is confronted and told that if it happens again there will be a consequence. Or, if the judge needs to make a point, the judge addresses the lateness by telling the participant that he/she needs to write and read an essay on respect at the next court session.

What kinds of behavior will result in termination from the program? Being re-arrested for a serious crime will result in termination, but sometimes it happens because of repeated relapses, being thrown out of treatment, threatening a member of the team, etc. Although Drug Courts usually give participants a number of chances, when it becomes clear that the team is more invested in the participants' recovery than the participant is, or when giving a participant another chance affects the credibility of the program, it is time to pull the plug. I have heard court officers say, "Who do you have to kill to get kicked out of Drug Court?"

Professional development and training are for the entire team. Each team member has to know the functions of other team members.

It is important that non-treatment members of the Drug Court team have a basic understanding of treatment, addiction, sobriety, recovery, etc. Treatment needs to understand the disciplines of the other team members and how they fit in with the rest of the team. This interaction is extremely important to the success, or lack thereof, of the program.

Training teaches that people addicted to substances go through a number of changes, known as Stages of Change, in their journey from addiction to recovery. It is important for the entire team to understand this process in order to adequately address the treatment needs of the participant at any particular time.

Treatment deals with all of these stages and has techniques for motivating the participants to advance to the next stage and to work with the participants to determine relapse triggers, so as to avoid relapse at each stage.

Training educates the team about medication-assisted treatment (MAT), which is the use of drugs that will assist in the participant's sobriety. Medication, such as Methadone, Suboxone, Buprenorphine, Naltrexone, and Vivitrol, are utilized in most drug courts.

Methadone is a synthetic analgesic drug that is similar to morphine in its effects but longer-acting, used as a substitute drug in the treatment of morphine and heroin addiction.

(Buprenorphine) Subutex is intended for use at the beginning of treatment. It helps fend off withdrawal symptoms that occur when you stop using opioids.

Naloxone (Narcan) is a short-acting drug, which will bring a patient out of an opiate overdose by stripping the opiate from the opiate receptor, and is a life-saving drug.

Suboxone contains a combination of buprenorphine and naloxone and intended for the maintenance treatment of opiate addiction.

Naltrexone (Vivitrol) blocks the effects of opioid medication, including pain relief or feelings of well-being that can lead to opioid abuse. Trexan is the oral medication and Vivitrol is the injectable medication.

I was initially opposed to the use of these drugs by our participants. However, I came to realize that addiction was a brain *disease*. If we treat physical diseases like diabetes with drugs like insulin or Metformin, even though people's lifestyles may have contributed to this disease, why shouldn't we treat this brain disease with certain drugs?

MAT certainly has its place to help people recover. In some cases, it is necessary for addicts to stay on those drugs for a long period of time even though you try to wean them off.

One of the main problems contributing to the opiate epidemic is the lack of MAT and physicians who can prescribe those medications. This country needs an easy-access system of urgent care centers that triage the addicted and, when they're ready, funnel them into MAT programs.

As a member of the faculty of the NDCI, I helped train numerous new drug court teams from Mississippi, South Dakota, Wisconsin, New Hampshire, Oklahoma, and other states. Over the last 30 years, there have been numerous research studies done on best practices, sanctions and incentives, and other important aspects of drug court practice. While the faculty was charged with teaching best practices, I felt my role on the faculty was to both teach best practices but also to give the new teams the benefit of my experience on a practical, not theoretical, level. For example, best practices provide that jail, if it is to be used at all, should be limited to a few days to a week. I had no issue with the research that supported such practice. However, when a judge is faced with a serious violation of the rules, such as forging self-help meeting lists, being arrested for a new serious offense, absconding, in my opinion, jail time of more than a few days to a week was warranted. For example, if a participant tested positive and did not admit prior to the test, he/she was committed to one week in the county jail, not for the use but for the dishonesty in not admitting. If the participant contested the test results, he/she would stay out of jail until the test was confirmed. If the test confirmed the previous test as positive, the participant would be sent to jail for two weeks—one week for lying on the original test and an additional week for putting us to the trouble of confirming the test when the participant knew he/she used.

I have no argument with the research, and support it in the vast majority of issues that occur in Drug Court. However, my experience is that jail can be a valuable tool for not only the participant offender but to all of the participants. Honesty is one of the keys to recovery. If you are not honest with yourself and with the team, you should be punished. Anecdotally, if you ask most of our participants what was the one factor that changed their behavior, they would respond that it was the time they spent in jail. They saw what their future would be if they didn't change their behavior. The issue is really *how much* jail is necessary to change behavior and whether too much jail does not work. Finding that happy medium is challenging.

CHAPTER 18.

Robert's Story

Robert spent a lot of time in Drug Court, both in in-patient facilities and being sanctioned to jail. His thanking his case manager, Ron Buster, was deserved. Ron, who recently passed away from cancer, was an extraordinary human being and was a recovering addict. He will be missed by me, his fellow case managers, drug court graduates, and the greater recovery community.

"First, I would like to thank God, for it is only through His grace and mercy that I am able to be sober today. I want to thank the drug court team, especially Ron Buster, who over a period of three-and-a-half years has been more helpful to me and to my recovery than anyone else. I not only see Ron as a counselor but more as a friend, with authority of course.

At this moment, I am being interviewed for the career that I've wanted since I was a boy, becoming a union steamfitter. This would not be possible if I was still using.

I will be forever in debt to Drug Court. If I did not have this opportunity to straighten my life out, I would not have had the chance to come in contact with the most important part of my life, that being God. It took a lot of fighting, kicking, and screaming to finally accept God. However, I finally surrendered my will and life to God and began the work to bring me closer to him on a day-to-day basis, which was when my life began to greatly improve. I discovered that the 12 steps are not steps away from drugs and alcohol as much as they are steps that bring you closer to God. My religious beliefs tell me that living a spiritual life is a life of taking action by showing God's love to all people, not just talking about it. How can I help a friend today? How can I help a perfect stranger today? I discovered that you can affect a person's life by showing compassion, which is a truly beautiful thing.

So now that I have ruffled enough feathers by talking about God, I am saying thank you once again and remind everyone that the path does not end here—it began with God and it ends with him. May his peace be with all of you."

CHAPTER 19.

Recovery and the "God" Piece

Robert's story is not unusual. Many in the early stages of recovery re-connect with religion. Most Drug Courts encourage and require participants to attend recovery meetings, have a sponsor, and study the 12 steps of AA. Why? We believe that engaging in recovery gives you the best chance of long-term sobriety. Most treatment programs encourage participants to do so as well.

There have been cases all over the country, however, where courts have held that you cannot compel individuals on probation to attend AA meetings, which engage in the functional equivalent of religious exercise, which is an action that tends to establish a state religious faith.

No one can truthfully argue that the original 12 steps of AA were not religious in nature. For example,

Step 3: "Made a decision to turn our will and our lives over to the care of God as we understood Him," or

Step 5: "Admitted to God, to ourselves, and to another human being the exact nature of our wrongs."

There is no real argument that there is a significant "God" piece in recovery.

How we dealt with this fine line was to inquire of the participant whether they had any deep-seated problem with the religious or spiritual nature of AA or Narcotics Anonymous (NA). If they did not, it was not going to be a problem. For those individuals who expressed such an issue, we recommended recovery meetings that were secular in nature.

I would also routinely mention that those who had those issues but liked the meetings except for the "God" piece, and were willing to continue attending them should ignore what upsets them and accept what else is offered.

I told them that whether their Higher Power was the Prophets Peter, Paul, and Mary, or the singing group of the same name, what only matters is that such higher power continues to keep them sober. Of course, some of the younger participants had never heard of that singing group.

Before I began presiding over the Misdemeanor Drug Court, it was suggested that I attend an open AA meeting. I did. I found it interesting and saw some people who I personally knew, but never knew that they were addicted and wondered whether they thought I was. During my time as presiding judge, I received invitations to attend celebratory AA/NA meetings from some of the Drug Court participants. I never turned down such an invitation, since it meant so much to those individuals for me to be there.

During court sessions, I would ask a participant how long their sponsor was sober, how often they spoke, and what step they were on. If they told me Step 8 (a list of the people they harmed), I would ask how long the list was. Most times they responded, "Very long."

After 12 years as a Drug Court judge, I believe that attending meetings, having a home group and a sponsor is essential for long-term sobriety, and I would urge the participants at graduation to continue to go to meetings.

CHAPTER 20.

Jeffrey's Story

Jeffrey came into Drug Court after having a fight at a bar celebrating his 30th birthday. He was intoxicated and when the police came and attempted to arrest him, he fled but was ultimately arrested and charged with assault and resisting arrest.

He came into Drug Court knowing that he needed to stop drinking since it was the cause of the incident. After successfully finishing Drug Court, he is now sober and has a successful career.

"The day of my 30th birthday was meant to signify the closing of one chapter of my life and beginning of a new one. It turned out to be a complete nightmare. I wished I was able to wake up from a terrible dream, but in reality, that dream was my reality. After a year of court appearances, I was allowed in a Drug Court program run by the honorable Judge Apotheker. I've heard plenty of stories about the man and how he would be harsh on people. The first day in court I observed how he operated. Everyone he was hard on actually created their own problems. In my personal opinion, I believed he was fair. If you didn't give him a reason to be hard on you, he would not have any reason to. From that moment on, I told myself I would do everything that is asked of me to help treat myself and become a better individual in the process.

In the beginning, it was very rough—the strict guidelines, programs, court appearances, etc. But as soon as I understood what the program was all about, things started to become clearer. Judge Apotheker would always reward and encourage me for staying on the right path. For the first time in my life, I was completely free from alcohol or any other kinds of drugs. I started to see everything clearly and slowly became the man I was destined to be all along. I was completely in control. Everything I ever wanted to do started to get done. I considered a career in real estate. That is something I was always interested in but never took action. I went to school and was granted my license and I have been practicing it ever since and now I am working on getting licensed in another state. I found what I like to do in life because I was sober. I thank Drug Court for that. If it weren't for Drug Court, I would have no idea where I would be in life. I thank Drug Court and Judge Apotheker for saving my life.

CHAPTER 21.

Drug Testing: Honesty, Creatinine, The Whizzinator™, and SCRAM™

Testing is the one of the most important parts of the program. You only know how participants are doing by testing them. I have often told participants that I would love to believe the words coming out of their mouths, but I know I can only believe the results from a test of their bodily fluids. Drug tests occur often and randomly. Most Drug Courts test for a wide variety of drugs as well as alcohol. The team cannot, under any circumstances, allow the participants to figure out when they may be called. We also have to consider their particular drug of choice and factor in the time it stays in their blood or urine. Marijuana, for example, stays in the system from time of use for approximately two to four weeks, opiates and cocaine, a few days, and alcohol, a few hours.

Most Drug Courts use a color or number method for random testing. A color and number are assigned to each participant. They are instructed to call at a certain time in the morning and if their color/number is on the recording, they must appear at the designated location and time to be tested.

Also, case managers can test at their meetings with the participants and participants can be tested in court as well.

Participants will often deny the results of a positive drug test. If the participant admits before the test, most judges will not sanction but address it in a treatment way. However, if a participant tests positive without admitting before the test, he or she may spend time in jail, not for the use, but for the *dishonesty* in not admitting it before the test. Honesty is an essential part of recovery and until you become honest with yourself and others, you will never find recovery.

If the participant denies, the sample is sent out for a 99.9 per cent accurate lab test. While it is being tested, the participant is not sanctioned. However, if it comes back confirmed, the participant spends extra time in jail for making us go to the trouble of sending it out when he knew that he used. As stated, I did not sanction for use. If someone comes in and tells us that they relapsed last night before the test, there is no sanction; we respond by adjusting their treatment.

There are a number of ways to cheat on a drug test and I'm not revealing any information that any addict doesn't already know. I have often said that I wished they spent more of their time practicing sobriety methods than they spent trying to get over.

The Internet contains numerous advertisements for products claiming that if you use this or that you are guaranteed to pass a drug test. My favorite is a product that offers a powder you mix with water. The powder is mixed with gallons of water and consumed over a period of time. What the amateur addict doesn't realize is that it is not the powder, but the water intake that attempts to flush the system and may prevent a positive result. Obviously, those who advertise this product wouldn't make any money if all you had to do is drink enough water.

Borrowing clean urine from someone who is not an addict and if you're a male, someone who is not pregnant, is another method. If you are a female, and borrow urine from another female, you might be surprised when you find out you are pregnant when the test comes back.

It is not as easy as it sounds. It's difficult to go up to a "clean" friend and ask them to pee in a cup for you. Then comes the next adventure, getting it past the person observing the test.

Yes, they are observed. Proper observation means staring at the participant's private parts to make sure that he or she is urinating from the proper places on their bodies. Sending a participant into a bathroom alone is both a waste of time and a test cup.

Picture this: you are a male with a small vial of borrowed urine. The first problem is getting it past the person observing the test since you must empty your pockets. Just think of the difficulty of trying to hide that small vile in one of your hands while pulling down your pants, and then holding on to your "Johnson" with the other hand, all while trying to pour someone else's urine from the vile into the test cup while looking like you are peeing in it, *and not be noticed!*

As stated above, there are many items on the market that will advertise that you will pass a drug test if you use the product. Many, if not most of these products, are mixed with a great deal of water that you are instructed to drink over a period of time. Drink enough water and you will dilute the sample.

There are two problems with flushing (drinking too much water). First, your urine will look like "Poland Spring," no yellow at all. For any seasoned "Urinator" or "Wiener Watcher" (as we named our male observer), the color should attract attention. Second, a lab test report should include a creatinine level.

Creatinine is a protein found in urine. A normal level is between 50 and 350. When a lab test of a participant comes back with a level of 20 or below, either the person is "water loading" (drinking too much water) intentionally or not, or is suffering from a health problem, serious enough to be hospitalized, or is from "planet creatinine," not from planet Earth.

When a participant observes Drug Court for the first time and when they plead into Drug Court, I routinely explained what creatinine is and how important the levels are. We would allow participants a number of low creatinine levels before we would terminate them from the program. With each low level there would be an increased sanction, and a warning to see their physician to see if they are sick. When they get to the fourth low level (20 or under), they are terminated from the program unless they can show a medical/scientific reason for the low levels. I have received many doctors' notes that try to support some disease that the participant may be suffering from, such as diabetes. My favorite was an excuse offered by a petite female whose doctor said that her low weight was the reason for the 20 and under levels. I inquired of the doctor to explain why there were perfectly normal creatinine levels after most tests, but low levels after some tests. Did this lady lose or gain weight? No, her weight was consistent. So what was the cause? Answer: she was water loading occasionally.

When her doctor couldn't show reliable scientific evidence of a reason or a disease, she knew she could no longer get over and was going to be terminated and sentenced to prison. Another Drug Court miracle occurred! Her low creatinine "disease" was cured.

We would use the same criteria to terminate if an individual's low creatinine levels were due to a disease, such as diabetes, as we would for those participants who medically require opioids. Since the participant's diabetes prevents us from properly monitoring creatinine levels, we would need to terminate that individual, with a non-jail/prison sentence.

We could not operate a legitimate Drug Court testing protocol without creatinine levels.

The Whizzinator™ is one of my favorite devices and, of course, advertised on the Internet.

This is a device mostly used by males. It's a device that has, on one end, a plastic bag filled with "toxin and disease-free" urine place under the armpit to keep it warm. A plastic tube connects the plastic bag under a male's armpit to an artificial penis. The artificial penis has a button on the bottom. When that button is pressed, it starts the flow of the urine from the plastic bag to the artificial penis and eventually into the testing cup. In a tribute to marketing, the artificial penis comes in six different colors to mimic skin color and a "Whizz Kit" with synthetic urine.

If a Drug Court does not mandate that males must drop their pants before peeing, they leave themselves open to the use of such a device. Let's assume that the color of the artificial penis matches the participant's skin color. But even if they try to use it, it is cumbersome. Most men will be nervous wearing such a device since they are told early on that if caught with this device, they will be terminated. Knowing that most men don't need to press anything to start peeing, the "Weiner Watcher," if he is paying attention, will then wonder why does this guy seem to be playing with himself? Busted!

Alcohol is a drug that quickly moves through your system and, therefore, challenging to test. One of the ways of testing is for the participant to wear a SCRAM™ bracelet. The bracelet is attached to the ankle. The bracelet is able to detect the presence of alcohol in the bloodstream 24 hours a day, seven days a week from the sweat on your ankle. If detected, it is reported quickly to the court. Can you avoid such detection? Yes, but it is quite difficult. With the SCRAM™, the only way is to place something between your skin and the device. However, when the device detects something obstructing it, a "tamper" is reported to the court, which then requests the participant to explain the "tamper." Usually, one tamper report and one visit to the judge convinces the participant to be "more careful!"

An ignition interlock device (IID) or breath alcohol ignition interlock device (BAIID) is installed in vehicles where the defendant has been convicted of a DWI-related offense. It works by the driver blowing into the device, which is then analyzed. If the reading is high enough, the car won't start. The device can also send a message to the driver that unless he/she pulls over within a few minutes and blows into the device, the car will shut off. If the driver does blow and the reading is too high, the driver will not be able to restart the car and police will be dispatched.

The technology is constantly improving. Within a few years, the IID will be able to analyze the sweat from your hands holding the steering wheel similar to how the SCRAM™ device now works. The IID is a tool that, in coming years, should be installed in every automobile manufactured *whether or not* the driver has been convicted of a DWI-related offense. It is a matter of public safety and prevention and until there are driverless cars, it could eliminate virtually every drunk driving incident and the needless tragedies that occur. We buckle up and cars have airbags to prevent or reduce serious injuries and death in traffic accidents. In the United States, 10,874 people, including 1,147 children, were killed just in 2017 as a result of drunken driving-related accidents. The installation of IIDs will reduce those tragedies dramatically!

In the last few years, an 80-hour alcohol urine test was developed. It was used when the SCRAM™ device was removed or when there was a suspicion that someone might be drinking.

CHAPTER 22.

Rachel's Story

Rachel was a young woman, who, while addicted, engaged in some dangerous relationships. Drug Court not only tries to get the participant sober, but aided by treatment, it also tries to suggest much more healthy ways of living your life.

"I want to thank you once again for the opportunity you gave me to enter the Drug Court program. In doing so, you gave me the chance of a lifetime to turn my life around.

As you know, when I first appeared in front of you, I was broken spiritually, physically, and mentally. And I was terrified that I wouldn't be able to complete the program. I felt this way because using drugs was the only way I knew how to live. In the end I needed them to live. Without the opiates I would feel so sick, and would do anything to get them, which is why I ended up in front of you.

The moment I was arrested, I was in shock and in total disbelief at how low I had sunk. I was ashamed that I let drugs take over my life, not allowing me to see any of the red flags or dangerous situations I put myself in. What I'm trying to say is that all morals were shot due to the power my addiction had over me.

But all that changed once I was accepted into the program because my secrets and lies were now in the light. The only person left to lie to was myself. Once I was given direction and encouragement, I was able to stop lying to myself. I told myself that this is my time to get better and that's exactly what I did. I remember you asking me what my goals were and I said I want to be drug-free and learn to make good choices and have healthy relationships. Little did I know that I would end of doing just that and more.

Throughout my time in Drug Court, I was able to learn coping skills, how to talk about my past traumas, and how to love myself regardless of my past mistakes. I really love myself for the strong woman I've become, Clean, Sober, Healthy, and Happy.

CHAPTER 23.

Building a Felony DWI Drug Court

In the Spring of 2008, with the full support of our district attorney and sheriff, we began to accept participants charged with felony DWI. I had been advocating for this move almost from the time I started as a Misdemeanor Drug Court judge eight years earlier.

In 2000, there was plenty of opposition to this program from local politicians and from inside my own team. One teammate had a family member who was killed by a drunk driver and did not want to see these individuals in Drug Court.

During that time, my team and I attended the annual conference of the National Association of Drug Court Professionals. It was there that I watched a lecture from Nadine Milford, president of Mothers Against Drunk Drivers (MADD) in New Mexico. She spoke about what happened to her family as a result of a drunk driver. She lost her only daughter *and* three of her grandchildren. If anyone had a right to feel that people who drink and drive should be treated harshly, it was Milford.

But instead of advocating for harsher penalties, surprisingly, she advocated for these offenders coming into Drug Court. She felt that this program could help prevent drunk driving and the tragedies that often occurred. Sure, some argue that these offenders belong in jail, but they eventually are released, and when they are released, they are still alcoholics and, therefore, still a danger to the driving public.

I had a chance to meet with Milford and arranged for her to meet with my team member who also lost a close relative. It had the effect of at least impressing upon us that while we might have misgivings, we should keep an open mind.

I asked Milford to write a letter to us in which she gave our community and our team the reasons to advocate for accepting DWIs into Drug Court. She wrote as follows:

June 13, 2000

Dear Judge Apotheker.

Being the State Chair of Mothers Against Drunk Driving in New Mexico means I have suffered a personal loss. On Christmas Eve 1992, my daughter and three granddaughters were taken from my family by a drunken driver. Since that time, I have become involved in every facet of MADD and have openly lobbied for changes in state laws. In the last seven years, we have, in fact, made New Mexico a safer state for our citizens and those who pass through, by passing legislation that reduced the BAC to .08, closed drive up liquor windows, and stiffened the penalties for repeat offenders. We have also raised awareness through a variety of programs, including education and prevention, public forums, and victim assistance.

My interest in Drug Court began when I sat on the DWI Oversight Task Force for the State of NM. This group proposed legislation for the governor's approval. Judge Michael

T. Kavanaugh invited me to assist in obtaining passage of this program with the DWI Oversight Task Force. I was not initially impressed, but later I attended the first meeting of Drug Court and additional court sessions with clients (i.e. drunk drivers). As I observed, the judge could be tough if they did not comply, and I watched him put people back in jail in order to keep the integrity of the program. A few months later, I attended a graduation of the maiden class. What I saw astonished me. These people had bonded with the probation officers and the judge. They hugged the parole officers and told the judge he had saved their lives. It was obvious to me that this program was making an impact and changing their lives and behavior. I was invited to be the keynote speaker at the second anniversary celebration. Many of these participants gave their testimony and were still clean.

New Mexico has been No. 1 in the nation for drunken driving crashes for years. In the year 2000, we are No. 4 in the nation per capita for fatalities. Drug Court definitely has had an impact on the drunken driving statistics in our state and, for the time being, we are dealing mostly with drunk driving.

As a victim of a drunken driving crash, it may seem odd to others that I would champion this program. The positive side is that I have seen the good that has come from Drug Court and feel confident it will continue to diminish our high statistics. If Drug Court continues to do the fine work that you are doing, then my workload with victims will be lighter, and maybe someday be eradicated.

Sincerely,

Nadine Milford

One of the serious problems that we faced in 2000–2001 was establishing a testing protocol for alcohol. Alcohol is a drug that is quickly metabolized in the system. Although there were some testing tools during that period, they were quite expensive and, in our opinion, not up to our standards of reliability to satisfy due process.

In 2007, when I resumed presiding over Drug Court, now as a felony level judge, I resumed my quest to bring DWI felonies into Drug Court, now with an acceptable and reliable method of testing for alcohol. It was the SCRAM™ bracelet that I discussed in Chapter 21. We nicknamed the bracelet "Brittany" and "Lindsay" for those celebrities that were required to wear them.

In 2008, with the letter from Nadine Milford, gaining support from the local MADD chapter, support of the sheriff and new district attorney, and a reliable testing protocol, we began accepting felony DWI participants.

Having the support of MADD was essential to gain the support of the local community. It also gave local politicians cover if a tragedy occurred, which never happened to this part of our program but always could. Not many district attorneys would take that risk, but DA Thomas Zugibe had the courage to take those risks.

Looking back, this became one of the most successful Drug Court programs, helping alcoholics stay sober and, at the same time, keeping the driving public safe.

The issue of undocumented immigrants coming into the DWI program became an issue as soon as we started it. At first, I was against them coming in. I felt that this was a program for

U.S. citizens and not undocumented aliens. It was a mindset similar to my close-minded opinions years before about Drug Court itself and MAT. I eventually came to the conclusion that these people lived and worked in our community, mostly in jobs that Americans didn't want to do. Some of these families have been living in our community for many years. One thing many of them had in common was a drinking problem that manifested itself in DWI arrests, which could result in deportation. These people presented a danger to themselves, their families, and to the driving public just as citizens did. We started taking them in with the understanding that they would be treated the same as citizens, with no breaks given to them because of their status.

Our experience was that the undocumented people in our felony DWI program on average did better than the citizens. Why? They had much more to lose. In many cases, a felony conviction for them meant certain deportation. We offered them a chance, if they were successful, to have that felony reduced to a misdemeanor, which reduced their chances of deportation. They didn't fear jail or prison. What they feared the most was leaving the country that they lived in for many years and never seeing their children again. *That* was motivation!

During that time, New York passed a law regarding DWI offenses when children were passengers in a vehicle driven by someone who was intoxicated. It was called "Leandra's Law" named for Leandra Rosado, an 11-year-old girl who was tragically killed in an accident caused by an intoxicated driver-friend of the family, in a carpool situation. Her father became involved in the passage of this new law, so that the death of his daughter would have some meaning and help prevent these types of occurrences in the future.

Normally, a first-time offense for DWI would be classified as a misdemeanor. However, under Leandra's Law, first-time offenders or not, if you had children under the age of 15 in the car while driving drunk, it was charged as a felony, with state prison with a possible sentence of four years (if the child was uninjured) up to 25 years (if the child was killed).

We had a policy of not accepting anyone in the program where an individual was injured as a result of a DWI offense. We decided to accept Leandra's Law offenders provided no injuries occurred during the offense. We offered the same downside and upside. Successfully finish this 18-month program and the class E felony would be reduced to a misdemeanor, and they would be sentenced to three years' probation. While in the program, they would wear the "Brittany" for six out of the 18 months, be in treatment, go to four AA meetings a week, see their case manager, and be subject to random testing for all drugs, including an 80 alcohol test when they weren't wearing the Brittany. This was not a walk in the park!

However, in late 2017, Leandra's father became angry that some counties in New York State were reducing the felonies to misdemeanors. It is difficult to make people who have suffered such terrible tragedies understand that programs such as ours reduce the chances of a tragedy. People like Nadine Milford are rare.

CHAPTER 24.

Damien's Story

Damien's story can be anyone's story. Upper middle-class professional family, bright student- athlete with a great future, who gets caught up in the drug culture and spirals downhill.

"Life is...for lack of a better word, unpredictable. The world, the people that inhabit this world, societal norms, and values are all ever evolving, yet for a majority of my young adulthood, I had genuinely believed that the world revolved around me. I was above authority, rules, and the laws that make up and govern our legal system and protect our civilization. In hindsight, I am aware that these misconceptions were just some of the character defects that would later be exacerbated by something much more powerful than I could have ever imagined. This delusional thinking grabbed me, like a mother's inherent desire to hold her child's hand, providing a level of comfort to repudiate any sense of a moral compass.

As an outsider looking in on my childhood, one would not understand how I could develop such a defiant mentality, having been raised by two morally sound, accomplished and well-respected parents. Having been adopted into a family of Ivy league graduates (my mother a college professor, my father a doctor) should have equated to a the same level of success naturally, as they provided me with financial stability, as well as countless educational and extracurricular opportunities, while instilling a strong work ethic and an open-mindedness to my perception of the world. This privilege, however, was overshadowed by my naivety, which I believe to be a common character trait for teens in my position. I felt a strong desire to deviate from the wants and expectations of my parents and teachers and pave my own path. I believed the delusions of grandeur telling me that I did not have to conform to societal norms in order to become a success. In my mind, I was already great, having become an accomplished and sought-after athlete, with an innate ability to connect people together through my "business ventures" as a promoter/marketer for NYC nightlife. It was those very thoughts that fueled my egotistical mentality, which would unknowingly propel me down a rabbit hole, for which I wasn't well equipped to handle.

Ironically, drugs and alcohol hadn't even been introduced to the picture at the time I began to exhibit these self-defeating traits. My childhood was filled with the pleasant memories of any typical suburban upper middle-class kid. School, soccer, music, friends, and family vacations were my biggest worries. In my teenage years, I recall spending a majority of it trying to balance school, sports, and social life, as it would naturally become a main priority for any high school kid to maintain some sort of socialization. What I was aware of in these moments of hanging with friends and chasing girls was the overwhelming feeling of discomfort and anxiety that, looking back in hindsight, stemmed from how I was perceived in the eyes of the people I interacted with. The emotions that come along with rejection, whether it be of a social circle or the girl you like that sits in the back of your math class, can be daunting...in fact, almost paralyzing. And so, I would allow it to dictate my life. It became easier to play it safe to avoid the forlorn feelings that would come with potentially putting myself out there and being misunderstood, or unseen or invalidated for being myself. I began to internalize this safety and began to lose confidence in who I was as a person.

The times that I felt most like myself and most alive were when I was playing sports. I found myself able to be free from judgment and it provided a platform to express the creativity that was yearning through my veins. And so, I trained...I trained hard! The hard work began to pay off as I began to rise through the ranks of every team I played on. By my junior year of high school, I was ranked the top player in New York State's Olympic Development Program.

Colleges began to reach out to me, interested in recruiting me. I was gaining attention from people all over and the really enjoyed the recognition for my abilities. I began to realize that sports was my path.

By my senior year, externally, everything was good. I was thriving in sports, doing decent in school, and increasing my social circle through my job as a promoter of teen nights at nightclubs in New York City. Internally, I was still struggling with the uncomfortable feelings of being accepted for who I was beyond the surface level. The pressures associated with maintaining a "cool" image for my peers and how teenage guys and their social status were heavily influenced by their ability to attract members of the opposite sex began to inundate my conscience. With prom season approaching and college nearing soon after, I knew something had to change within me to surmount the anxieties I was faced with.

The first of several proms I went to that senior year was the one that stood out to me the most, as it was that night that would unknowingly change me in ways I could have never imagined. I was attending the prom of a neighboring high school with a girl who I had dated briefly throughout my last year of high school. The prom went off without a hitch...the traditional gathering for prom pictures before being picked up by a limo, arriving to a beautifully decorated event space at the lavish hotel, the speakers pumping out the Top 40s of that time period with colorful lighting filling the room while we danced the night away, and the hugs and high-fives as the prom culminated and everyone prepared to get ready to head to the city for the after party.

Back in the limo and en route to Manhattan, the excitement permeated the dark tinted, elongated luxury vehicle. One of the passengers in the vehicle opened up his bag and pulled out a bottle of vodka and some colorful light yellow pills that, upon closer examination, were imprinted with a sun on them. There was a clear sense of excitement, as everyone in the limo started cheering at the sight of what was in the bag. Through the cheers and elation, my friend leaned over and asked:

"You want some?"

"Sure why not?" I replied as calmly and cool as I could respond.

"All right D! Here you go," he said as he handed me the oversized bottle of Grey Goose and an Ecstasy pill.

But truthfully, I was scared. I had never drank or ever taken any type of drug in my life. But I also knew I didn't want to be "that guy" who wasn't cool enough to join in on the fun. And so, apprehension aside, I grabbed the bottle, took a couple swigs, and popped the pill that was handed to me. I had no idea what to expect, what I was supposed to feel, or what was going to happen to me. And so, I just waited and tried to act accordingly in congruence with everyone else in the limo.

We arrived at the nightclub in Manhattan. It was a nightclub called the Sound Factory, renowned for their over-the-top parties that could go all weekend. As we entered the club, I recall feeling very relaxed. Any anxiety or tension from the limo ride had been alleviated. A warmth had fallen over me. I felt…free. And with that feeling of freedom, I partied, I mingled, I flirted, all for the first time with a sense of courage that I had never felt before. I didn't understand what I was feeling, but I enjoyed it. For the first time in my life, I felt like I could be myself without any judgment.

The rest of the night was a complete blur to me. I can't remember what time we left, what time we got home, or even how we got home. But I can recall waking up the next morning and wanting to do it again. I was unaware that the event that fateful night would lead me down a dark rabbit hole in the years to come.

That night became the theme for my existence for the next few years as I entered college. Playing for a Top 25 ranked Division 1 program, I struggled balancing school, sports, and my social life. Things began to really spiral out of control as I found myself sidelined for every single game. For the first time in my life, I wasn't the star of the team. Hell, I couldn't even make the starting lineup to be in a position to play. Frustration and disappointment began to set in, mixed with arrogance and a strong distaste and defiance towards the coach for not recognizing my ability. And so, I decided that I would show the coach by refocusing my attention away from the team and going all in on the social scene at my school. I didn't want to face or address the anger or depression I was feeling from not playing. So, to numb those feelings I drank until I blacked out, and I used various drugs to avoid blacking out once I realized I couldn't handle alcohol on its own. But most of all, I avoided feeling the discomfort of my reality—that I wasn't doing the one thing I loved to do in my life.

The year flew by, and by the end of my freshman year, I found myself kicked out of school for poor grades and poor attendance, a clear indicator to some, that I may have a problem. This became a reoccurring theme, as I found myself kicked out of yet another school the following year, and again at the local community college the year after. I was unable to manage any sense of consistency in the classroom, yet the one thing that remained consistent was my incessant need to drink and drug. I didn't see a correlation between my partying and my school record, nor did I view it as a problem. I didn't even want to be in school! And that is how I justified my behavior. This justification made it much easier for me to decide that I no longer needed to be in school and could pursue a career as a DJ in the very same nightclubs that I continuously partied in every weekend. This would be my calling and I would become a world-renowned DJ, touring the world, sharing the gift of electronic music to the masses.

I dedicated my life to learning the craft of DJing. I practiced seven to eight hours a day, downloading music, and developing and honing my craft. I spent my time in nightclubs partying but also networking and getting close with the promoters that had the power to book me when the time was right. I had reconnected with some old friends from high school who, like me, were avid nightclub-goers and together we infiltrated the circle of the biggest DJs in NYC. Finally, the opportunity presented itself for me to get my break and DJ my first gig. After that first gig, came another gig…and then another gig…and then another gig. I eventually found myself building a name for myself in the greatest city in the world as a DJ. I was gaining momentum and recognition from people all over the industry. My dream was coming true. I knew that I was on the right track to make my dreams come true.

As my dreams of becoming an established DJ was coming to fruition, the closest of my friends were engaged in building their own empire, for lack of a better word. With the nightlife industry commonly associated with club drug use, my friends saw an opportunity to capitalize on the market. We were now very well known throughout the industry, so naturally they took advantage of this and began to profit off the sales of illicit drugs. And with drug selling came heavier drug use. The types of drugs were generally the kinds you would normally find in a club setting—cocaine, ecstasy, and ketamine. But one day, while at one of their homes, I was presented with a small blue pill that was very different from what we normally would ingest.

"Dude, just break this in half and take just the half," said my friend Jay.

"Well, first off, what is it?" I asked.

"It's a roxy" he replied

"What the hell is a roxy?"

I responded bewildered by the name of the pill.

"It's a painkiller. Just trust me ... you will love it!" he asserted, as he broke the pill on the computer desk by his bedside and handed it to me.

Within 20 minutes of ingestion, I felt an indescribable feeling overcome me. The only thing I could comprehend happening to me was this was exactly how I wanted to feel all the time. And so began the chase of the magic dragon. I began to take the pills more regularly and within a very short period of time, I found myself inundated with the idea of wanting to feel like I did all the time when I was under the influence of this magical, little blue pill. Without the pill, I felt lethargic, almost sick at times, unaware of the repercussions that came with long-term use of an opiate. It got to a point where I could no longer wait to get my hands on them through my friends and realized I would need a doctor in order to obtain my own batch to prevent me from getting sick.

Uncertain of how I would be able to convince a doctor that I was in need of a prescription of Oxycodone, I concluded that it would be in my best interest to take it upon myself to create my own prescription. Fortunately, with my father being a well-respected doctor, I had access to an unlimited number of prescription pads that he had, innocently and unknowingly, left around the house in case immediate family members needed an antibiotic or some non-narcotic prescription. And so, through heavy research on the Internet, I learned how to write my own prescriptions. I also learned necessary diagnosis codes and common doctor/pharmacist terminology, in case I would have to act as the prescribing physician over the phone to verify a prescription.

This was before the times of electronic prescriptions and connected pharmacy networks, and so it became a game (in hindsight more like a job) of keeping track of prescription fill dates and pharmacy locations that would work more easily in filling my prescriptions. But it worked! I became as addicted to the thrill of duping unsuspecting pharmacists as I did to the actual drug. The feeling of invincibility fueled my ego, as I saw no chance of me getting caught. This went on for some time until one fateful Sunday morning. I had filled a script, unaware that they had contacted my father, who told them he had not written the prescription.

About a month after the day I filled that prescription, I awoke in the same fashion I would any other day. It was a typical late Friday morning for me at the time, though that's not the case for me anymore. Dressed in the same black Puma sweatpants and my favorite slightly discolored, white Abercrombie & Fitch hoodie that I had been wearing for the past two days, I had just crushed up and sniffed my last blue [the street term for Oxycodone] and lit up my second to last Marlboro Light cigarette. The smoke began to permeate the room, accentuating the little sunlight coming through the rectangular basement window, as my friend Matt entered. Matt, a kid I knew from high school who was now a drug dealer, had been evicted from his apartment for some unknown reason, and I, who was fortunate enough to have taken over my parents oversized two-bedroom basement, jumped at the opportunity to have him move in with me. How much closer to the source of my drug habit could I get than having a drug dealer reside in my house, right?

Matt sat on the couch across from mine and proceeded to mimic my aforementioned actions. There was always excitement in what seemed like a ceremonial process: the folding of the dollar bill, the crushing of the blue in the bill with two coins (quarters seemed to always be most efficient), the rolling of the second dollar bill, the sniffing of the crushed blue powder, and lastly the lighting of the cigarette in culmination. There was a twisted beauty in the process, which was purely insane when I reflect on it now.

I had the TV remote in my hand and was perusing through the available movies, enjoying the last few pulls off my cigarette, as the warm, euphoric feeling of the blue coursed through my body like an oversized comforter on a cool winter night. But the feeling was ephemeral. Its *effects* had become less and less *effective* every passing day I got high, forcing me to do more and more, chasing the feeling of that first time I had ever tried that nefarious little pill. "What would I give to relive that first high..." was a constant thought that consumed me daily.

We decided to watch the newly released *Hunger Games: Mockingbird* movie. I remember being excited to watch it since I had missed it in theaters. Like many activities I had once enjoyed, going to the movies was no longer a possibility now that all my money went towards the drugs I was using. As a result, I generally found myself confined to my basement. My limited social interaction included only the few drug addict friends who would stop by to buy their pills from Matt. Little did I know that those interactions and moving Matt into my home would have dire consequences attached to them.

The movie started, but despite my anticipation, I was unable to focus on the heroic tale of Katniss Everdeen. All I could think about was where Roger was and how long until he arrived at my house, so that Matt could re-up on his supply of pills. That was generally my thought process when I ran out of blues—impatiently wondering where and how I would get the next pill to support my habit. I asked Matt what Roger's ETA was when I heard a thunderous knock at the door, followed by the crazed sound of barking from my little black and white Havanese dog named DJ. I swear DJ thinks he's an overprotective, 150 lb. Rottweiler when someone is at the door. But the little guy is all bark and no bite. I jumped up, realizing it's hard to hear the doorbell from the basement. Maybe it was Roger, who stupidly went to my front door when I told Matt to tell him to go around back to the basement door, or maybe it was the UPS guy needing a signature for one of the hundreds of packages my sister always has delivered to the house. Either way, "I had better hurry upstairs and answer the door," I thought to myself. I sped up the flight of steps, skipping every other step like I had always done as far back as I can remember. Reaching the landing to the first floor, completely out of breath, all I could think was: "Fuck, I need to stop smoking!" Still out of breath, I made my way to the front door and reached out to open it when...

The door flew open, almost as if set to an automatic timer. Before me stood over a dozen individuals holding guns that looked like they belonged in the final standoff against Tony Montana in *Scarface*.

"PUT YOUR HANDS UP AND GET ON THE FUCKING FLOOR!" demanded the first of three SWAT team members. Scared and confused, I complied with his order as men dressed in black tactical gear, police uniforms, and navy colored jackets with the letters D.E.A. on the back entered the house. Instantly, I was thrown to the floor and handcuffed. The cold metal of the tightly bound handcuffs on my wrists sent chills up my spine. As I laid there helpless, I just watched black boots begin to parade through my parents' house. I could hear them make their way up the dual staircase to the upstairs bedrooms, some stayed on the main floor, tearing through rooms, while the remainder made their way to the basement. This wasn't my first run-in with the law, but I knew this was much more serious than anything up until this point.

I was finally lifted up by one of the few DEA agents and placed onto a chair in the dining room.

He began to ask me questions and I proceeded to answer them, acting as if I had no idea what was happening or why they were there. But I knew. My actions over the past few years had led up to this moment. My addiction to prescription painkillers had set me on a destructive path, causing me to lose my moral compass. Deciphering right from wrong had been thrown out the window long ago as I began to steal and write prescriptions from my father, the loving and caring man who, with my mother, adopted me and provided me with numerous opportunities to succeed in life—all to support my drug habit. At this moment, I knew that the gig was up.

By July of that year, I found myself standing in front of a man, dressed in a black cloak with a very stern demeanor sitting at a bench in an over-sized, modern looking courtroom. To my right stood a gray-suited public defender that had a dozen or so manila folders, some thicker than others, labeled with various first and last names of offenders he was assigned to represent. I had spent the last several months attempting to get my charge of possession of a forged instrument dropped completely, but due to some prior arrests, the District Attorney's office refused to let me go without me being held accountable for my actions.

Not feeling well due to opiate withdrawal, I had yessed my way through a series of questions my representing attorney had asked me regarding my understanding of what Drug Court was, what was expected of me, and the ramifications of any illicit behavior that happened between this day and my day of completion. Thereafter, I re-emerged from a small backroom into the courtroom, and pled into the 18-month Felony Drug Court program, run by the very same judge.

I knew very little about Judge Apotheker, the presiding judge over the Felony Drug Court program. I had heard him address the Drug Court participants that day I pled in, and recall him emphatically discussing the importance of honesty. The only thing that resonated with me at that moment was how honest my feelings of disdain for him were. I had no desire to learn anything about him or hear anything he said to me, or any participant. To me, my only interest was finding out the easiest way to get over on the judge, his staff, and anyone else I would encounter through this process that could potentially hinder me from continuing to use the drug that landed me into this mess to begin with.

My first task as the newest participant of the Rockland County Felony Drug Court program was to enroll in the Lexington Day Treatment Outpatient, as assigned per my case manager, Harriet Carter. This essentially meant that I would attend a five-hour a day out-patient program, addressing the underlying issues of my addiction, while being monitored via drug screenings three times per week. This was on top of the series of random drug screenings that would be issued by the Drug Court program itself, through their color/number protocol. It became apparent very quickly that this would be a much harder task to getting high than I had anticipated.

I had made the decision that Friday that I was going to quit cold turkey and do what I had to do to get through this program as quickly as possible. But unaware of how insidious the disease of addiction was, I found myself running the streets of NYC with my drug dealer, two days later getting high without any care or concern of what would be in store for me as a result of my actions.

By the end of that evening, I found myself being driven to Good Samaritan Hospital, involuntarily, to avoid having to be remanded for using over the weekend. I had done a couple of days in jail before and was well aware of how un-enjoyable the experience was, so admission into a 28-day in-patient rehab program seemed like the lesser of two evils.

I arrived to the hospital and was escorted to a small room where I was forced to wait for several hours. While I sat in a hospital bed awaiting my admission to the rehab, I was overcome with trepidation, fearing the experience that I was about to embark on. I had never envisioned my life coming to this point. Rehab was for people with drug problems! And I clearly didn't fit the bill as a drug addict in my mind. My thoughts began to shift from where I was presently to the nefarious activities that I would do the second I got out of this rehab.

Finally, at 2 a.m., I was admitted into the rehab unit, known as 5 North. And my rehab journey began. The days were filled with various groups addressing issues related to drug use, the effects of various drugs on the body, identifying potential triggers that could result in relapse, educational videos about the experiences of others and AA/NA meetings that were brought in through various outside groups. There was absolutely nothing that I was able to identify with. I was completely close-minded to the entire experience and couldn't relate to anything that was being presented to me. This negative mindset, combined with a very stubborn and arrogant attitude, led to my eventual discharge for violation of several rules of the in-patient program. So much in fact, that the director of the in-patient program wished me the best of luck with my "bullshit," when I would have to go back before the judge.

Completely unaltered by her pitiless words, I was free from the confines of the rehab unit I had been locked away in for the last three-and-a-half weeks. I had come close enough to completing the program that I couldn't imagine the judge doing anything other than admitting me back into the out-patient program I was briefly in, and

I could finally go and get high like I had planned from the day I was admitted into the in-patient rehab facility.

"The defendant is to be remanded for one week," were the shocking last words of Judge Apotheker, just before I was whisked off by the court officers behind a closed door, where I was searched, handcuffed, and thrown into a small holding cell while I awaited to be transferred to the county jail. I could not comprehend what was happening to me. I had practically completed the in-patient program. How could this judge not deem that as acceptable and let me go back to living my life?!

Within days of entering the county jail, I soon learned, through my case manager, that I would have to go through another 28-day in-patient program, plus they would be increasing my level of treatment, forcing me to endure an additional 90-days of in-patient treatment at yet another facility. Unbeknownst to me, this would be an ever-changing experience that would alter me in ways I couldn't have imagined.

Prior to arriving at the 90-day treatment program, I had experienced another hiccup in my journey and, again, found myself remanded back to the Rockland County Jail. Fortunately, I was able to get a bed at a facility at a treatment program renowned for their spiritual-based approach to the disease of addiction. I had no understanding of spirituality and was very turned off by the idea of God or religion and so I couldn't imagine the facility having any effect on me. But it was the very same misconceptions that I held walking into the facility that afforded me the opportunity to change my heavily distorted thinking and embark on a new journey. Through my experience at St. Christopher's Inn, located in Garrison, NY, I grew introspective and was able to face many of the underlying issues that

I had compartmentalized for many years with the help of my drug use. I began to gain a new perspective on my life and began to value the second chance that I was being given through this program. Most importantly, I began to love myself again... something I hadn't been able to do for a very long time.

My paradigm for living shifted in my time on that magical mountain. I returned to civilization, upon successfully completing the program, with a new mindset and attitude toward how I wanted to live my life. I saw, for the first time, that I had a purpose greater than the miserable existence that I had succumbed to for the years leading up to my arrival into Felony Drug Court. Judge Apotheker could see the change as well. His overwhelming sense of compassion and recognition of this change in me filled me with joy. For the first time in my life, I felt as if someone else saw the potential that I was finally seeing in myself. He became my biggest supporter, week in and week out, reminding me of the terrible condition I was in early in my time with Drug Court. His fear of my imminent death was now turned into positive, reassuring conviction that I could break the grips of addiction, and embrace sobriety and all the gifts that it promised, without the constant reminder that it will be a lifelong battle...one that would not be easy.

I was reminded of the insidiousness of the disease through the many unfortunate overdoses I was forced to witness over the next couple of years. Individuals that I had either known prior to getting arrested or that I met through my journey into recovery became motivation as "Rest in Peace" posts on social media appeared all too frequently. I began to understand the severity of what I was dealing with, and made a pact with myself to use the deaths of my friends and acquaintances as motivation to rise above the epidemic that was taking the lives of countless Americans by the hour.

I had also begun, subconsciously, to take interest in the very same legal system I had found myself intertwined with. Upon my completing an associate's degree at the local community college, I had also been exposed to law through two business law classes, where I thrived and really began to explore the possibility of pursuing law as a career. Today, I am very blessed to have continued to maintain my sobriety and further my education, currently in line to complete my bachelor's degree this upcoming spring semester, with plans to pursue law school and hopefully provide the same inspiration that Judge Apotheker instilled in me in my journey through his Drug Court program. The idea of rising from the darkest of places that any human could imagine emotionally, physically, and spiritually, and turning a negative experience into one where I could potentially help numerous individuals who find themselves in the same position that I once did, would be the most gratifying experience of my life. And I am forever grateful for the experience of Rockland County Drug Court, and being able to build a relationship with Judge Apotheker. Without him and the Drug Court experience, I would have unquestionably become another statistic of the opiate epidemic."

Recently I was honored by a local alcoholism center. I asked Damien to introduce me. He was perfect and it affected everyone in the room. At the end of his introduction, he thanked me. I mentioned him in part of my remarks.

"I picked Damien to introduce me because I knew he would be a great speaker and his story is special. During my 12 years as a Drug Court judge, there were many successes like Damien's, but there were also failures, resulting in prison and those who tragically died of overdoses. Like many who enter Drug Court, Damien was a mess, needed jail to motivate him, and, after a long time, became a person you see today. I am so proud of him and many others that I still keep in contact with, some of whom are here tonight.

Damien invited me to his college graduation; he graduated Magna Cum Laude. I had not been the Drug Court judge for over two years, but Damien, Joan, and many others are constant reminders that Drug Court made miracles.

April 30, 2020

I sit here looking at the Hudson River on a cold, rainy morning during this pandemic, about to send this manuscript to the publisher. I spent three years, on and off, working on this book. Hopefully, you have enjoyed reading it, and learning about Drug Court and my contributions to it.

As youngsters, most of us wonder what we will become, what will we grow up to be? Many of us are disappointed, wished we would had accomplished more, or taken a different road.

At the age of 53, I finally found what I wanted to do when I grew up.

I am happy and healthy, have a wonderful family, and trying to avoid Covid19.

I feel most fortunate.

CHAPTER 25

The Most Important Advice I Can Give to Readers

Over the years, I have spoken to many parents who have children addicted to substances asking my advice on what they should do. I told them what they did not want to hear. If you suspect that they have drugs in the house, or on their person, call the police. If they steal from you, have them arrested. Don't bail them out of jail. Get a lawyer for them who is pro-Drug Court and try to get them in.

While it may be the toughest thing a parent can do, it just may prevent you from having to do something much tougher—arranging for their funeral.

APPENDIX

Appendix A

More Information about Drug Court

NADCP's website: https://www.nadcp.org/

National Drug Court Institute: www.ndci.org

Other organizations providing scholarship, training and technical assistance for Drug Courts and other treatment courts:

Center for Court Innovation: www.courtinnovation.org

Children and Family Futures (family drug courts):www.cffutures.org

Council of State Governments Justice Center: csgjusticecenter.org

Justice for Vets (Veterans Treatment Courts): www.justiceforvets.org

Justice Programs Office at American University: www.american.edu/spa/jpo

National Center for DWI Courts: www.DWIcourts.org

National Center for State Courts: www.ncsc.org

National Council of Juvenile and Family Court Judges (juvenile and family drug courts): www.ncjfcj.org

Organization of American States (international treatment courts): www.oas.org

SAMHSA's GAINS Center for Behavioral Health and Justice Transformation www.samhsa.gov/gains-center

Tribal Law and Policy Institute (Tribal drug courts): www.home.tlpi. org

The 2016 Painting the Current Picture Report is the most up-to-date review of research on the effects of drug courts and other treatment courts, and the state of the field as of 2015. https://www.ndci.org/wp-content/uploads/2016/05/Painting-the-Current-Picture-2016.pdf

The Best Practice Standards describe how Drug Courts should operate to achieve the best outcomes:

Volume I: https://www.nadcp.org/wp-content/uploads/2018/12/Adult-Drug-Court-Best-Practice-Standards-Volume-I-Text-Revision-December-2018-1.pdf

Volume II: https://www.nadcp.org/wp-content/uploads/2018/12/Adult-Drug-Court-Best-Practice-Standards-Volume-2-Text-Revision-December-2018-1.pdf

The Multisite Adult Drug Court Evaluation (MADCE) was a nationally representative study proving that drug courts work: https://nij.ojp.gov/topics/articles/nijs-multisite-adult-drug-court-evaluation

10 Key Components

The Drug Court Ten Key Components

Key Component #1: Drug Courts integrate alcohol and other drug treatment services with justice system case processing.

Key Component #2: Using a non-adversarial approach, prosecution and defense counsel promote public safety while protecting participants' due process rights.

Key Component #3: Eligible participants are identified early and promptly placed in the Drug Court program.

Key Component # 4: Drug Courts provide access to a continuum of alcohol, drug, and other related treatment and rehabilitation services.

Key Component #5: Abstinence is monitored by frequent alcohol and other drug testing.

Key Component #6: A coordinated strategy governs Drug Court responses to participants' compliance.

Key Component #7: Ongoing judicial interaction with each Drug Court participant is essential.

Key Component # 8: Monitoring and evaluation measure the achievement of program goals and gauge effectiveness.

Key Component #9: Continuing interdisciplinary education promotes effective Drug Court planning, implementation, and operation.

Key Component #10: Forging partnerships among Drug Courts, public agencies, and community-based organizations generate local support and enhance effectiveness.

12 Steps

THE TWELVE STEPS OF ALCOHOLICS ANONYMOUS

Step 1: We admitted we were powerless over alcohol—that our lives had become unmanageable.

Step 2: Came to believe that a Power greater than ourselves could restore us to sanity.

Step 3: Made a decision to turn our will and our lives over to the care of God as we understood Him.

Step 4: Made a searching and fearless moral inventory of ourselves.

Step 5: Admitted to God, to ourselves, and to another human being the exact nature of our wrongs.

Step 6: Were entirely ready to have God remove all these defects of character.

Step 7: Humbly asked Him to remove our shortcomings.

Step 8: Made a list of all persons we had harmed, and became willing to make amends to them all.

Step 9: Made direct amends to such people wherever possible, except when to do so would injure them or others.

Step 10: Continued to take personal inventory and when we were wrong promptly admitted it.

Step 11: Sought through prayer and meditation to improve our conscious contact with God, as we understood Him, praying only for knowledge of His will for us and the power to carry that out.

Step 12: Having had a spiritual awakening as the result of these Steps, we tried to carry this message to alcoholics, and to practice these principles in all our affairs.

Appendix B

Saving Rockland Lives Editorial

Saving Rockland lives

Drug Court has impressive record of doing that

When a life is literally saved in substance-abuse treatment, there is joy, relief and watchful waiting.

For a recovering addict is just that, a lifelong addict, who though he or she may never use alcohol or drugs again, has temptation for a constant companion. It is personal courage, continuing, effective treatment and community support that keep the person clean and proud of his survival.

It is in that vein that we congratulate the 10 new graduates of Rockland's Drug Court, a most humane effort to save lives and to spare society the grief and expense and pain of more drug-related crime and even loss of life.

Recently, as reported by staff writer Steve Lieberman, the graduates used pride, humor and tears to express their strong will to remain drug- and alcohol-free.

To earn their right to stand on a Haverstraw podium before judges, prosecutors, police, counselors, family and friends, each of the 10 graduates spent up to two years in drug treatment. All were nonviolent offenders with substance abuse addictions who chose treatment instead of jail or prison.

"Drug Court gave me my life back," Demetrio Mendez, 41, told about 75 people attending the court's fifth graduation, held at the Italian-American Club. "I have been clean and sober for 16 months. I have a job. I am getting my GED (high school equivalency diploma). I got my respect back, and I got my family back."

While each of the graduates and more than 30 people still in the program had lived under different circumstances before Drug Court, Mendez's life was typical: addicted, unemployed and with a criminal history. Participants have lost their families, their jobs, their self-respect. They had come to hate themselves and to spew that venom toward others.

Drug Court offers people a chance to get off substance abuse and to accept a most challenging, lifelong battle to remain clean but with this great reward: a purposeful life filled with family, a job, self-respect.

The court does more than turn lives around. It saves money in incarceration and associated welfare costs. And it allows police and other law enforcement to address other crime and our basic safety needs.

It helps the ordinary taxpayer, not only in cost savings but in fewer victims of such crimes as burglaries and driving while under the influence.

Mendez said, "I hope I can stay like this. I still got my mind; I don't want to lose my family again." He most certainly can stay clean, as so many have. He can do that knowing he has his loved ones' support as well as the community's. May he know that more people are pulling for him than he can possibly imagine, the same sort of seemingly hidden, good humanity that revealed itself so openly and fully in the heroism of Sept. 11.

With this week's ceremony, 39 people have graduated from Rockland Drug Court since it was established in January 1998. Special state legislation allowed the countywide court to be overseen by town judges, first by Clarkstown Justice Craig Johns and then by Haverstraw Justice Charles Apotheker for the past two years. In March, Apotheker will turn over the Drug Court to County Court Judge Kenneth Resnik, most qualified by his many years on the bench as a Ramapo town justice.

The Drug Court team includes prosecutors, defense lawyers, mental-health officials, substance-abuse counselors, probation officers and police. The court is one of about 30 such courts operating in New York, Judith Kaye, chief judge of the state, wants the courts extended to every community. We second that.

A state commission appointed by Kaye found that only about 15 percent of participants in 20 state drug courts had been rearrested one year after their graduation, compared with about 35 percent who had been rearrested one year after leaving jail or prison or after being placed on probation. Of all of Rockland's Drug Court participants, 95 percent have graduated; just four have been rearrested.

One reason, experts say, is that treatment helps addicts change their lifestyle, including getting more education, new housing and a job. Also, a Drug Court participant is constantly monitored, meeting weekly with the judge. Participants are subject to in-patient and out-patient care, and random and scheduled drug testing.

Judge Apotheker noted that each graduate represents the aspirations of Drug Court, as well as the people taking the program. "You have enriched my life in a way you cannot imagine," he told graduates.

Yes, that is what happens when you do good.

2003 Graduation Remarks

Thank you for that kind introduction. Even though it is bitter cold outside I am warmed by seeing old friends and that I get to participate in a very important event in Rockland county—not only for the graduates and their families but for this community. When I presided over these graduations, I was always gratified to see community leaders, elected officials, and representatives from the treatment community. All of us in this field know that Drug Courts can only be successful by having widespread public support. While the graduates and their families benefit from this program, who can quantify the benefits to our community when these graduates stop committing crimes, save money by not being in jail, get jobs, education, housing, so they can get off welfare, reunite with their families, get custody of their children and have drug-free babies. Yes, Drug Court graduations are important days in Rockland and all of you, the entire Rockland community, should be proud of your hard work in bringing this about.

Today, I'd like to speak about change—change in people's perceptions about Drug Court, change in how I came to view this program, and, most importantly, change in the behavior of the program participants.

Recently, the Center for Court Innovation published its evaluation of the various Drug Courts in New York. They studied nine different Drug Courts, some in New York City, and some in suburban and rural locations. The study found that those in Drug Court had a 29 per cent lower probability of re-arrest and it indicated Drug Court participation produced lasting changes in the participants, and that graduates have far lower recidivism rates than those not in drug courts.

Simply Drug Courts Work!

But I wasn't always a fan. I had my doubts in the beginning, but started to change my mind when I went to my first Drug Court graduation and saw the transformation of the participants. I was moved by the stories, which caused me to volunteer in 2000 to bring the Misdemeanor Drug Court to the Town of Haverstraw, where I continued to be moved by the stories of addiction, sobriety, and recovery. During the two years I served, 45 people graduated with the vast majority having not been re-arrested.

When I presided over my own graduations, many of the graduates would tell me how grateful they were. Having graduates and family members thank me for saving their lives is very sobering (no pun intended). Although this is a team effort, we can't underestimate the power of the robe to be a force for positive motivation. I did struggle in the beginning though. I had trouble making a connection with the participants. It was Patti who suggested a "makeover"—that I needed to make physical contact with the participants when they did something positive. It helped me to not only make the participants feel that I cared but I also really started to care. And like parents care for their children, establishing limits, praising them when they deserved it but with that ever present 2' by 4' to whack them upside the head to get their attention, I changed!

Although the judge gets a lot of the credit, the truth is that Drug Courts are really effective when you have a team of competent and dedicated people. People like ADA Beth Finklestein, ADP Lois Cappelletti, Coordinator Judy Rosenthal, and Case Managers Ron Buster and Patti Rogers. There is really only one word that comes to mind when I think of Patti. No, the word isn't stubborn. The word is irreplaceable.

One of the improvements I have recommended is bringing in DWI offenders. It has worked in many jurisdictions, even getting the support of some MADD groups. We also need to have random testing on weekends and home visits. There is also value in seeing whether we can accept low-level non-violent drug sellers if the seller is also addicted. We may see that we can get both the seller and the buyer off the street.

Our Drug Court is still in the toddler stage and we can't stand pat. We need to grow with the needs of our community, change when we have to, and stay innovative.

But this day is about the graduates and I remember most of them and how they changed from the time they came in to the time they graduated.

I remember Barbara who invited me to an AA meeting to help celebrate her one-year anniversary. I remember feeling terrible having to send Theresa to jail for eating a poppy seed bagel even though I knew inside that she didn't use, but the rules had to be followed. And to Theresa's credit, she also knew I had to do it but didn't want to. I also remember Artie who died tragically and was much too young.

Early on, Patti gave me some good advice. "Don't get too excited about the successes or too disappointed about the failures." I have passed on the advice to many other Drug Court judges. The problem is when you change from being detached to being involved, following that advice is easier said than done.

I mentioned earlier how moved I am when the graduates tell me that I helped them. Seeing the physical and emotional condition of the people that leave the program compared to how they came in, and knowing that I played an important part in changing their behavior for the better has been the most rewarding and satisfying thing I have ever done. And every Drug Court judge will say the same thing.

Advice to the graduates: Keep your focus. Stay in recovery. Don't stop going to meetings. Keep in touch with your sponsor and, of course, People, Places and Things.

Thank you all very much for not forgetting me, and inviting me to share this special day with you.

Drug Court judge sees 'power of recovery'

(Original Publication: January 14, 2007)

It was close to midnight on Election Day and the returns in the race for County Court judge were looking pretty solid.

That's when veteran Haverstraw town Justice Charles Apotheker moved outside, onto the steps at Pasta Cucina in New City, where Democrats were getting the good news on races from the village level all the way to the governor's office.

The news that night included the election of Apotheker and Clarkstown Town Justice Victor Alfieri Jr. to County Court, defeating two Republicans - Karen Riley and Barbara Gionta - who had been appointed to the bench in June by Gov. George Pataki. They succeeded William Kelly, who had been elected to the state Supreme Court, and Kenneth Resnik, who had retired.

And there was Apotheker, on the front steps of the restaurant, letting Resnik know he had won.

It was Resnik, after all, who had urged him to run for County Court, Apotheker explains. It was Resnik who knew why Apotheker wanted the job and it was Resnik who wanted it so much for him.

For Apotheker, who served 26 years as Haverstraw's town justice, wanting to be a county judge wasn't about prestige, a higher salary or a longer term.

Something had been missing for Apotheker since the county's Drug Court shifted from a rotation through the town courts to come under the jurisdiction of the County Court.

From 2000 to 2002, Haverstraw hosted the Drug Court under special legislation that made it possible for other Rockland towns to transfer their nonviolent drug cases there.

The point of Drug Cour -, a concept Apotheker admits he initially opposed - is to offer drug offenders an opportunity to avoid jail by pleading guilty and entering into a rigorous program of treatment, counseling and monitoring. If they are successful, graduation from the program means the charges are either dropped or greatly reduced.

It was attending one of the first Drug Court graduations that changed his thinking. "You saw how behavior could change, given the right stimulus," he says.

The goal is for those who pass through the Drug Court to remain free of drugs, and also remain free of the legal problems and family and career issues that go along with abuse and addiction.

"You see the power of recovery and the alternatives that are out there to jail," Apotheker says, explaining that Drug Court makes heavy demands in return for the opportunity to stay out of jail. Participants are required to take part in a treatment program, report to court, attend several self-help meetings and meet with case managers who are part of the Drug Court team - all on a weekly basis. On top of all that, there are both scheduled and random drug tests.

Apotheker emphasizes that Drug Court's success comes from its team approach, involving a coordinator, prosecutor, public defender, social worker, police and others, but says the key is the judge's role.

"I'm a social worker with a 2-by-4," says Apotheker, who like other town judges could only hear misdemeanor drug cases at the justice court level. "When you have a felony," cases that move to County Court, "that becomes a 4-by-4."

It's up to the judge, with the help of the team, he says, "to create an environment where they know they can't get away with anything."

Because drug addicts facing felony charges in County Court risk substantial prison time, he says, there's all the more motivation to plead guilty and do what's required by Drug Court, including find employment and housing.

The benefits for the participant are a life free of drugs and legal problems, and a chance at a stable family life.

The bottom line, Apotheker says he tells participants, is that "you get to live instead of dying."

According to numerous studies, the benefits for society include far fewer repeat offenders, less stress on the prison system and fewer drug-addicted newborn babies.

Apotheker was so successful during his time presiding over Drug Court and became such an advocate for the alternative to jail that he was asked by the state Office of Court Administration to help train other judges to preside over similar courts in their jurisdictions. He's also on the faculty of the National Drug Court Institute and has helped train Drug Court judges around the country.

When Drug Court was leaving Haverstraw and shifting to Rockland's County Court, it was Apotheker who trained Resnik, his friend for 30 years.

While he understood the logic in shifting Drug Court out of town jurisdiction, he knew it meant that the only way he could preside over it again would be to run for County Court.

It was Resnik, who moved from Rockland after his retirement, who convinced him to make the run.

And it was people he's encountered in the community who convinced him - without even knowing it - that he had made the right decision.

While walking streets in Congers with his wife to gather signatures for his nominating petitions, Apotheker approached a family sitting on the steps of their home. "You're the Drug Court judge?" he recalls one of them half saying and half asking. "He said his son was doing well and thanked me."

Later, while campaigning outside Rockland Bakery in Nanuet, he had a similar experience when a man approached him to thank him for helping his son turn his life around.

"I can't take full credit - ever," he says in relating the story. "I'm just the daddy. I wear the robe and have that 2-by-4."

In a couple of weeks, Apotheker takes over from Family Court Judge William Warren, who has been running Drug Court. Apotheker will be trading up to a 4-by-4. He's already discussing adding a police component to the Drug Court team with Sheriff James Kralik and hopes someday to expand the court's scope to also address alcohol addiction.

Although elected to County Court, Apotheker initially will be presiding in Family Court here and in drug courts in the city of Middletown and Putnam County, where he'll help train new judges to take over.

"Being a Drug Court judge is exhilarating, disappointing and exhausting," Apotheker says, "but it gives you a sense of accomplishment that nothing else does."

2008 Christmas Card

2008

Dear Judge Apotheker,

Merry Christmas! How are you? We are all doing great. I wanted to send you some pictures of my family. Holly, who is 6, and my twins who are 1! This year I will be celebrating _8 years clean & sober_, all thanks to you and the staff of drug court. God Blessed all of us! Frank will be celebrating 3 years clean and sober as well. We are very happy. Take care.

Remarks at Drug Court Graduation, January, 2018

Judge Russo, Thank you for inviting me today as your guest speaker.

It's been almost 13 months since I last presided over Drug Court. I would be less than honest if I said I didn't miss it. I do. And yes I am detoxing from this very slowly. But what I miss the most is working with this team of true professionals. Since 2004, as a member of the faculty of the NDCI, I have mentored many Drug Court teams all over the US, but I can truthfully say that this team has the most talented and knowledgeable people that I have ever had the pleasure of working with. They care about you and want you to succeed and do everything they can to help you. And this piece of advice I gave to judge Russo— they know what they're doing and the few mistakes I made was when I didn't follow their advice.

And by the way, thank the police officer that arrested you. They started you on the road to your recovery.

I have admitted that I really miss this, but I have also said that the only constant in life is change. Change happens and you have to adjust. So I'm back practicing law and continuing to help addicts who get into trouble. Recently, I told Patti what I was doing and she said, "So you were a social worker judge and now you are a social worker attorney." Guilty!

I am also writing a book about my experiences as a Drug Court judge that will include some of the letters that I have received over the years from Drug Court participants, some of which were written to me from jail. No one's names will be used, but some of the stories are very compelling. If any of you want to be part of this I invite you to write your story and send it to me. Apothekerlaw@ gmail.com.

One story that will be in my book I will share with you today. I was having some renovations done to my home earlier this year. A young man working as a meter reader for the water company knocked on my door. He was looking for the owner of a car parked outside. I thought it belonged to the contractor and called him to come downstairs. While we were waiting for him, the young man said I looked familiar. He asked what I did for a living. I told him I am an attorney now, but I was a judge. He said, "Judge Apotheker", I said yes. He said, "Can I give you a hug? You saved my life 15 years ago." He told me that he was a member of a gang in Haverstraw, addicted and going down the wrong path. He got sober, left the gang, and is still sober 15 years later. How did this happen? How does someone looking for the owner of a car, not knowing where I lived, not even looking for me, randomly knock on my door and find me?

In the years doing this, the program has had many, many successes and some tragic failures. Trying to figure out why some succeed and some die or go to prison is almost impossible. I used to call it fairy dust, but most of it has little to do with the program and much to do with the participant's effort, mindset, and mental health. Why does someone whose behavior was so bad that it resulted in my calling her a junkie, turn it around, graduate and become a valued member of the community? Why did two people who I put in jail go on to get their CASAC and Social Worker degrees, and are now drug counselors? Why does a beautiful 20-year-old girl die of a heroin overdose within one week of being released early from prison? Why does a Drug Court graduate who had not a sanction during his time, did everything expected of him, go out on a boat one dark night and kill two friends because he was high? Why do Americans consume the vast majority of opiates in the world? And why have we lost 60,000 people to drug overdoses last year, more than all the soldiers killed in the Vietnam War that lasted 15 years. And why, after declaring a national opiate epidemic public health emergency a few months ago, has not a dime been appropriated by the government?

I wish that all of the experience I have had would give me those answers, but it hasn't.

What I do know is that your chances of having long-term success increases with your willingness to stay connected with recovery.

This year is the 20th Anniversary of Rockland's Drug Court and we're hoping to have a celebration at this summer's graduation. While not forgetting those who didn't make it, we will celebrate the hundreds of participants who succeeded and are doing well, including all of you who graduate today. And I wish all of you much success.

Most of you will remember that if a participant came to court with a baby I had to hold him or her. I had to hold them for two reasons. One, it is very significant in the Drug Court field to have sober babies born. In fact, statistics for this are recorded. And two, I was a grandfather deprived.

But no longer, 11 weeks ago, on election day, finally, my first grandchild was born and he is a joy. I wish to share with anyone who wants to see pictures of the most beautiful baby.

Thank you for inviting me.

Remembering Justice Marshall

Recently, the Rockland Human Rights Commission inducted a number of worthy individuals into the Civil Rights Hall of Fame. One of those was the late Thurgood Marshall, associate justice of the U.S. Supreme Court.

That day, Cecilia Marshall, Justice Marshall's widow, attended the ceremony and luncheon in Nyack. Being the only individual in the room ever to have appeared before Marshall, it brought back memories of the Supreme Court case that I was directly involved with as co-counsel (with Marc Parris, the county attorney at the time) for the County of Rockland.

Thurgood Marshall was the template for equal justice for all people. Through his courage and great legal skill he brought numerous and successful legal challenges to segregation. His most famous success was Brown vs. Board of Education when the Supreme Court finally overturned the doctrine of "separate but equal." This distinguished legal career led to his appointment as the first black U.S. solicitor general and later as the first black associate justice.

What I didn't know in December 1979, when we were preparing for the argument in our Supreme Court case, was the connection that Marshall had with Rockland. During the argument I was slightly puzzled when one of the other justices asked where Rockland was, and it was Justice Marshall who answered. Some years later I learned that in the 1940s he had successfully challenged Hillburn's segregated school system.

I was fortunate to have a few minutes with Mrs. Marshall at the luncheon. I told her that I had appeared before the court while her husband was sitting there. She told me that each day, before her husband left for the Supreme Court, she would tell him "Thurgood, don't be mean to the lawyers." I told Mrs. Marshall that while he had not been "mean" to me, he became quite angry when our adversary misquoted him.

Our case involved the failure to rehire two assistant public defenders when the county Legislature's majority party changed from Republican to Democrat. It was our position that the political patronage system in Rockland should be allowed to continue so as to appoint young attorneys, no matter their gender or ethnic background, to positions such as these, which would prepare them for future elective office. At the time we didn't realize that Justice Marshall wouldn't be impressed with such an argument since in his life experience political parties often discriminated and were often closed to people of color.

Mrs. Marshall is still a vibrant and interesting lady who thanked me for sharing my experiences. Truth be told, I was the one grateful for the good fortune of meeting her.

Charles Apotheker
Haverstraw
The writer is town justice, Haverstraw.

In addition to firefighting . . .

I would like to express my sincere thanks to Bill Tarrantino, lieutenant of

Appendix C

Dr. Reginald Archibald

In Chapter 2, I made reference to the fact that I was sexually abused by a "reputable" doctor. I decided that I would "come out" and the following is a copy of the article appearing in the *New York Law Journal* on June 5, 2019.

Accountability for Rockefeller University

Hon. Charles Apotheker, former Acting New York State Supreme Court Justice

When revelations came to light that Dr. Reginald Archibald, a well-respected pediatric endocrinologist at the Rockefeller University Hospital, had spent decades sexually abusing young boys under the guise of medical "treatment," I was flooded with memories that I thought were tightly sealed away in a mental box from 60 years ago.

When the hospital's own attorneys released a report last week confirming that Rockefeller University officials knew about the abuse but allowed it to continue, I got angry. I remembered being taken to a hospital by my mother and being led into an examination room by this white- haired doctor. I remembered being alone with Dr. Archibald and being told to take off all my clothes. I remembered being placed against a wall naked with my hands extended out towards him. And then I remember the picture-taking. Pictures of my naked 13-year-old body, followed by measurements of my penis. Then it all went blank.

Until recently, claims against Rockefeller University in New York State would have been timed-barred by law, blocking victims today from bringing actions against perpetrators of past child sex abuse.

However, the passage of the Child Victims Act now allows adults who were abused as children to renew these claims and finally hold institutions that served as breeding grounds for predators to account for their role in enabling and covering up the crimes of those they protected. And while recent legislation will provide a limited opportunity for victims of Dr. Archibald and Rockefeller University to file a civil action, it's also time for the Manhattan District Attorney to launch a full-scale investigation, starting with its own investigation in 1960, about who knew what and when, and who made the decision to cover it up.

For a long time, I used the distance of 60 years as a mental barrier to an otherwise traumatic event. But recently, I have become angrier. The false comfort that six decades brings has been tossed aside knowing that there are pictures—unaccounted for—that memorialize the trauma Dr. Archibald brought upon me. These are pictures that Rockefeller University has yet to account for, but now admits that they exist.

As a parent, I am also angry about the guilt my parents would have felt had they known that they had allowed their son to be abused by this monster. Recently, I received my medical records from Rockefeller and in them there was a consent form, signed by my mother, that stated: "I hereby consent that any 'routine' procedure of 'minor' operative character, that may be deemed necessary, may be performed upon my son." What was an otherwise routine document was used as a sick permission slip to violate a child.

Throughout my decades-long career as a judge, I buried my own trauma as I came across victims in court who had faced similar abuse. I never told anyone what happened to me—not even my parents. But for the sake of justice I cannot stay silent any longer.

There is still pain.

Pain in knowing that there are pictures out there, unaccounted for, of a 13-year old me that were used, not for medical purposes, but for the sexual gratification of an institutionally protected pedophile.

Pain that Rockefeller University still has not revealed the complete truth about Dr. Archibald and the investigation it claims to have conducted 15 years ago.

Pain I carry for my parents, who, had they lived, would have been racked with guilt for allowing this to happen to their child.

Pain in knowing that there are many former patients of Dr. Archibald who took this trauma with them to the grave, and many more who would have gone to the grave without obtaining justice and closure had the Child Victims Act not passed.

Pain in knowing, as an experienced judge and attorney, that Rockefeller University and their insurance carriers are capable of continuing to abuse us, this time as senior citizens with limited life expectancies, in a cynical attempt to run out the clock, so that many of us will never see justice done.

Just as Michigan State University knew what was happening in their own institution and did nothing to stop it, Rockefeller University also knew and did nothing. The University has now admitted liability in their public statements, writing, "We profoundly apologize to those patients who experienced pain and suffering as a result of Dr. Archibald's reprehensible behavior." But apologies and half-hearted internal reports are simply not enough.

Maybe we won't live long enough to see the results of a full-scale DA investigation, but I can tell you this—this retired judge and hundreds of other victims are now more motivated than ever to stay healthy and to live long enough to see justice done.

I have received many comments about it and much support. Although I would like to be remembered for the work I did as a Drug Court judge and all the people that I helped, it seems that I will also be remembered for "coming out" about child abuse as well.

ABOUT THE AUTHOR

Charles Apotheker was born in the Bronx, NY, attended local public schools, and graduated from DeWitt Clinton High School (1964). He is a graduate of CCNY (1968) and St. John's University Law School (1973). Judge Apotheker is also an honorably discharged veteran of the U.S. Army Reserve.

Judge Apotheker was a Rockland County Assistant County Attorney from 1974 to 2003.

He was Counsel to the Board of Ethics and the Budget and Finance Committee, among other duties. As an attorney, Judge Apotheker appeared before the Appellate Division's Second and Third Departments, the New York State Court of Appeals, the U.S. District Courts, and the United States Supreme Court.

Judge Apotheker was elected town justice of the Town of Haverstraw in 1979 and served for 27 consecutive years.

Judge Apotheker was appointed as Rockland County's Misdemeanor Drug Court judge in March 2000 and served in that capacity until February 2002, when Rockland's Drug Court was transferred to the county court.

In 2004, Judge Apotheker was appointed to the faculty of the National Drug Court Institute. Since that time, he has mentored numerous Drug Court teams throughout the United States. He has also lectured at the annual Conference of the National Association of Drug Court Professionals. In addition, he has served as a facilitator for the Office of Court Administration at state drug court trainings and as a member of the Statewide Drug Court Strategic Planning Committee. He has been a peer reviewer for Drug Court-related grant applications for the Bureau of Justice Affairs of the United States Department of Justice.

In 2006, Judge Apotheker was elected as Rockland County court judge. He was soon appointed as an acting justice of the Supreme Court and as supervising judge for the town and village courts in the 9th District, supervising 127 courts and approximately 250 town and village justices. At that time, he was appointed as Rockland's Felony Drug Court judge. During his term, the population of Rockland's Drug Court rose from approximately 40 participants to nearly 100 and the minority population in Drug Court significantly increased, reflecting the diversity of Rockland County.

Since leaving the bench at the end of 2016, Judge Apotheker was Of Counsel to the law firm of Phillips and Millman. In January 2020, he was appointed as Rockland County First Assistant District Attorney in charge of the Alternative to Incarceration programs.

He has been a resident of Rockland County since 1972 and currently resides in Piermont, NY, with his wife Francine. They have two adult sons, Jeremy and Lee, daughters-in-law Randi and Ariane, and grandson Asher Ilan.